The Modern Nations in

Historical Perspective

ROBIN W. WINKS, *General Editor*

The idea of the nation state, which has dominated
Europe since the French Revolution, now serves
the entire globe. To the resultant profusion of
political units the historian must bring perspective,
both to re-emphasize the universal quality of nationhood and to help make clear the diversity and
particularity of national experience.

The volumes in this series deal with individual
nations or groups of closely related nations, sum-
marizing the chief historical trends and influences
that have contributed to each nation's present-day
character, problems, and behavior. Recent data are
incorporated with established historical background to achieve a fresh synthesis and original
interpretation.

The author of this volume, SINNAPPAH ARASARAT-
NAM, is a native of Ceylon. He has studied at the
University of Ceylon and at the School of Oriental
and African Studies of the University of London,
where he received his Ph.D. The author of *Dutch
Power in Ceylon 1658-1687*, he is at present Senior
Lecturer in Indian Studies at the University of
Malaya in Kuala Lumpur.

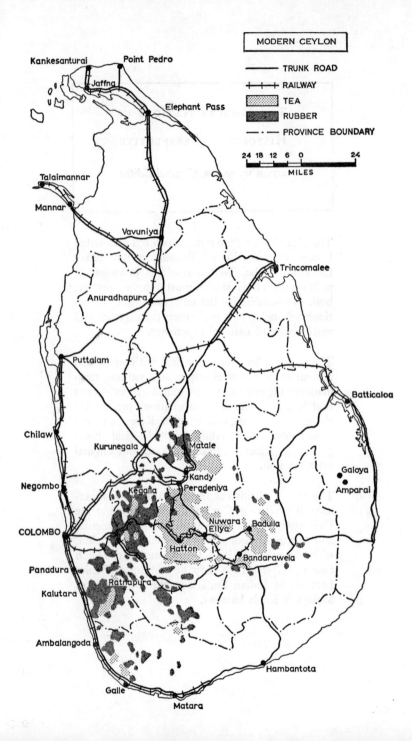

TRUNK ROAD
RAILWAY
TEA
RUBBER
PROVINCE BOUNDARY

24 18 12 6 0   24
MILES

Kankesanturai
Point Pedro
Jaffna
Elephant Pass
Talaimannar
Mannar
Vavuniya
Trincomalee
Anuradhapura
Puttalam
Batticaloa
Chilaw
Kurunegala
Matale
Galoya
Kandy
Amparai
Negombo
Kegalla
Peradeniya
Nuwara
Eliya
Baduila
COLOMBO
Hatton
Bandarawela
Panadura
Ratnapura
Kalutara
Ambalangoda
Hambantota
Galle
Matara

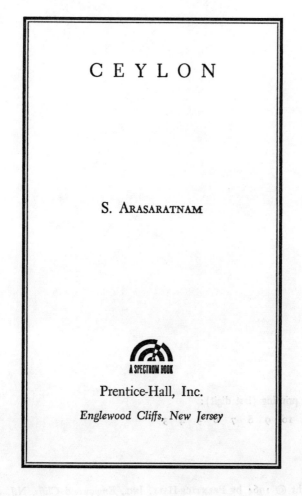

CEYLON

S. ARASARATNAM

A SPECTRUM BOOK

Prentice-Hall, Inc.

Englewood Cliffs, New Jersey

Current printing (last digit):

12 11 10 9 8 7 6 5 4 3

FOREWORD

Sri Lanka, the resplendent island of Ceylon, is less well known in Europe and the New World than its giant neighbor to the North, India, but its history holds equal fascination. As a member of the Commonwealth of Nations, Ceylon joins other Asian, African, and Western countries in a unique experiment within an international community of nations that wishes, through consultation and cooperation, to preserve ties which once were imperial only. The members of the Commonwealth—the United Kingdom, Canada, Australia, New Zealand, India, Pakistan, Ceylon, Malaysia, Ghana, Nigeria, Sierra Leone, Tanganyika and Zanzibar, Kenya, Malawi, Uganda, Zambia, Cyprus, Jamaica, Trinidad and Tobago, and Western Samoa—once were bound by the common bond of the British Empire. Today they are bound by a common desire to work out new, national destinies without turning their backs upon that past. Ceylon is crucial to this experiment.

Ceylon became independent in 1948 following 450 years of Portuguese, Dutch, and British rule. But Ceylon had an ancient culture of its own long before European contact with its gem-laden coasts; and, more than most recently independent countries, Ceylon continues to draw upon that ancient culture. No visitor to Sigiriya or Polonnaruwa, centers of ancient civilization, can fail to see that these ruins speak to the present in a way that those of Athens do (and those at Angkor do not). Ceylon is a seriously divided nation, rent by communal rivalries, by religious and political extremists, and by economic problems that seem to defy quick or rational solutions. But these problems are not entirely new, and much that pursues modern Ceylon arises from its long past.

The purpose of this volume is to examine Ceylon's modern crises in the light of that past. The volume is thus present-minded in its conviction that what is past is but prologue. But its author, Dr. Sinnappah Arasaratnam, also demonstrates clearly how far back into that past we must reach if we are to understand the present. Pathways to the present may be long or short; for Ceylon, as for India or China, they are unquestionably long. Thus, Dr. Arasaratnam devotes comparatively more space to the early history of Sri Lanka than has any other author who has set out to account for modern Ceylon.

The time has come for voices from within the Commonwealth countries to present their own accountings of their national histories, for only through the indigenous author may we gain the added dimension of hearing a sophisticated, scholarly, and yet nationally-oriented voice speak of those subjects that he, and not an outsider, considers important. The scholar must speak in the cadences of his nation, and in this Dr. Arasaratnam succeeds admirably. He is from Ceylon, and writes as one who is committed to his nation's importance must write. He is Western educated, an expert on the Dutch period of colonial rule, and he has travelled widely in the West. His is the first short history of Ceylon to be written by a scholar of either of the major indigenous communities of the country.

This book, meant not to replace but to supplement the longer text, is designed as an introduction for general readers, students, and hopefully statesmen, to one exceptionally meaningful, if confusing, national history. We live in a time of incredible and confusing change. As historians we must protect the canons of our scholarly objectivity and defend our interest in well-documented monographs. But we also have an obligation to write history so that our high school and college students respect the past for what it means to them today, so that they do not fear change, and so that they may understand and perhaps even anticipate change.

Robin W. Winks
Series Editor

The present work opens with a survey of the problems facing contemporary Ceylon and then outlines briefly the two and a half millennia of this island's history in order to explain, in part, the historical causes of the present dilemmas. The historical outline deals, first, with the three major communal groups that have over the ages made the island their home. Two of them are linguistic groups and the third a religious one. The Sinhalese, as the largest single community, occupy the bulk of the account; sketches of the two minority communities—the Tamils and the Muslims—follow.

With the period of European impact, the basis of treatment changes. From the sixteenth century the problems of Ceylon may be seen from the vantage point of the three European powers that colonized the island and influenced its history. There is, of course, an implied interpretation here; before the coming of the Europeans one must look at Ceylon's history in terms of the rise and growth of particular communities. In the colonial period an all-island treatment is plausible. An external hand seems to impose a degree of unity or at least provide a unified framework of development.

It is obvious that this study has drawn lavishly from several recognized authorities and specialist writings on Ceylon. To these generations of scholars the author acknowledges a deep debt of gratitude.

S. A.

CONTENTS

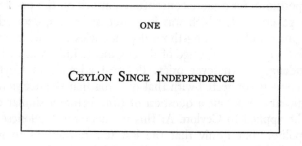

ONE

CEYLON SINCE INDEPENDENCE

THE ADVENT OF INDEPENDENCE

During the course of the Second World War, while defending her extensive empire in Asia, the British government sought to come to terms with nationalist forces in her dependencies of South Asia. Attempts were made in both India and Ceylon to negotiate a settlement of the constitutional problem with nationalist leaders and to give stability to the administration and strengthen the war effort. In India these protracted negotiations were a failure, because there was little common ground between the demands of the nationalists and the concessions proposed by the British. Disagreement between the two sections of the nationalist movement—the National Congress and the Muslim League—complicated matters further. Similar efforts in Ceylon fared better, for the demands and attitudes of the nationalist leaders were more moderate, and the proposals of the British government were accepted without much ado. Both parties were agreed in principle as to the next step; the Ceylonese leaders, who were holding ministerial office, drafted a constitution along lines which were known to be agreeable to the colonial government. The process of reform was set in motion even while the war was on, and in July, 1944, a commission was appointed, with Lord Soulbury as chairman, to examine the draft of the Ceylonese ministers, to receive other representations, and to recommend a constitution for Ceylon. The Soulbury Commission drafted a constitution that gave the island self-government in all matters of internal jurisdiction, retaining some safeguards to the British government in defense and the conduct of external affairs.

By the time the commission reported, the war had ended, and there was opportunity for a more concentrated attack on the problem. The Labour government, which was in power in Britain, decided to initiate a process of liberating those dependencies that were politically in a relatively advanced stage of development. India was to be given independence at whatever price. Political advance in Ceylon had been so closely connected with that of India that the decision to free India meant it was but a question of time before a similar decision would be applied to Ceylon. At this moment the Ceylonese leaders urged politely but firmly that the last few restrictions to independence imposed by the Soulbury Constitution be done away with. The British government was receptive to these requests. It was convinced that the leaders with whom it negotiated and who were likely to hold power in Ceylon for some time to come would be friendly to British interests. A decision was taken to confer dominion status on Ceylon. The few powers reserved in the Soulbury Constitution for the imperial government were also transferred to the Ceylonese legislature. These changes were incorporated in the Ceylon Independence Act of 1947.

The constitution of independent Ceylon was modeled largely on the British constitution. It introduced the system of parliamentary government as evolved in Britain and extended to the other self-governing dominions. It was rather different from the experimental system of government by executive committees introduced by the Donoughmore Constitution of 1931. By that constitution executive and legislative functions had been vested in a single body. In the British system executive power rests in the hands of a body chosen from and responsible to the legislature; the two functions are kept separate. The legislature of independent Ceylon was bicameral and comprised the House of Representatives and the Senate. The House of Representatives was directly elected by popular vote, and the Senate was in part elected by members of the popular House and in part nominated by the governor-general. The only restrictions to the power of lawmaking were the safeguards written into the constitution against discriminatory laws against particular religious or communal groups. The governor-general occupied a position akin to that of the British monarch and exercised similar constitutional functions. He was appointed by the British sovereign on the advice of the prime minister of Ceylon. His chief constitutional function was the appointment of the prime minister, who was called upon to form a government on the basis of the electoral results as reflected in the House of Representatives. He summoned, prorogued, and dissolved Parliament. All executive acts performed by the ministers were done in his name. In a country where the party system had not been defined with the clarity and precision it had in Britain, the governor-general had some measure of influence in the appointment of the prime minister and in the general conduct of affairs.

After the prime minister was appointed from the largest political grouping in the lower house, he selected his ministers, who were then officially appointed to their positions by the governor-general. These ministers together formed the Cabinet, which was collectively responsible for the government of the country. Their power was sustained by a majority in Parliament; if they lost that majority, they would have to resign their offices. The conventions observed in the conduct of affairs within the Cabinet and in the relation between Cabinet and Parliament were those of the United Kingdom. Proposals put forward by a minister were scrutinized and passed by the Cabinet and became the collective decision of the government. Legislation to give effect to these proposals was drafted by officials and presented to Parliament, where the government majority ensured its passage. On assent by the governor-general, it was enacted as law. As in the United Kingdom, both by convention and by law, the attempt was made to separate the political section of the government from the administrative. The appointment, promotion, and dismissal of government officers of a higher grade was under a Public Service Commission which was directly responsible to the governor-general. It was thus theoretically impossible for the ministers to interfere with appointments to the public service. A similar Judicial Services Commission functioned in relation to officers in the country's judiciary.

The constitutional structure set up was thus a ready-made and comprehensive one and provided the machinery for a smooth transition from colonial rule to independence. It was a structure with which the Ceylonese leadership was familiar, if only through the pages of textbooks on the British constitution. Though the previous constitution operating in Ceylon had not been quite so closely modeled on these principles, some of the elements of the parliamentary system were already there. Most of the politicians who were preening themselves to take power in the new dispensation had already acquired considerable experience in political affairs. The political institutions being Western, and the conduct of affairs mainly through the medium of English, it was the English-educated intelligentsia that produced the political leaders from the time that these representative institutions were introduced. Electoral results show that even the most remote rural districts chose members of this class to represent them in the legislature. The largely illiterate or semiliterate peasantry that formed the bulk of the population were not in a position to put up leaders of their own class and therefore had necessarily to choose members of the urban middle class who came forward and offered themselves as leaders. Some of these men had the added advantage of having previously functioned as ministers under the old constitution and thus had already grappled with problems of government. A few of the leaders at the top had handled the delicate negotiations with the imperial government and had so impressed the latter by their qualities of statesmanship that even without popular clamor for independence the British government was persuaded that the Ceylonese could now manage their own destiny. All this experience was to be a great asset in the process of working out the new constitution and the fully self-governing status it conferred.

These new leaders had a common background of English education, though they came from widely different walks of life. Some of them belonged to the old landowning aristocracy and still held considerable land in their constituencies. They thus enjoyed the influence that went with their traditional family connections and had equipped themselves for leadership in the new age by imbibing the new ideas that the Westerner had brought. A totally different group was the "new rich," those who had benefited from the economic opportunities opened by the British and had emerged as a native entrepreneur class with varying degrees of success. The rest belonged to the different professions, all of which had involved study of the English language. Predominant among these were the lawyers, who, as in contemporary India, provided more than their share of recruits for political leadership.

The common educational background and the values and ideals they shared gave homogeneity to this new leadership. Fundamentally, Ceylonese society was divided into a plurality of communal and religious units. These units were certainly not, at this stage, hostile to each other, nor did they have very much in common with each other. One could talk fruitfully of a Ceylonese nation only in terms of the English-educated intelligentsia. At this level, both socially and intellectually, took place the mixing of communal groups and the merging of communal differences. This westernized elite rose above the divisive factors in society and indeed gradually presented themselves as yet another of its many component groups. The one advantage was that its members were drawn from all parts of the island, all language groups, and all religions. They ran the administrative services of the country, taught in its schools, and strongly supported the political leadership of their English-speaking compatriots. Together they would ensure the smooth working of the new political institutions and the pursuit of certain ideals which they would seek to impart to the mass of the people.

In the process of making the constitution, a separate organization was formed to represent the interests of the Tamils. This demanded a formula of balanced representation to safeguard minority communities against domination by the Sinhalese majority. This organization, the Tamil Congress, was popular in North Ceylon, where the Tamils were concentrated. But many members of the English-educated section of the Tamils dissociated themselves from the Tamil Congress and grasped the hand of friendship offered by the Sinhalese. Furthermore, leaders of other minority communities willingly offered their cooperation to the Sinhalese. In the first Cabinet of independent Ceylon, all the major communities were represented.

Compared to the other countries that secured release from British tutelage at about the same time—India, Pakistan, and Burma—Ceylon's economic situation may be described as sound. The average income of about 300 rupees per person per annum at this period compared favorably with that of most other Asian countries except Japan. The plantation sector of the country's agriculture was doing well and fetching good prices in world markets. Tea, rubber, and coconut —all in good demand in world markets at that time—were the major exports and provided about 90 per cent of the country's earnings of foreign exchange. No doubt, during the war much of the rubber had been slaughter-tapped to meet immediate needs, but there were great possibilities for future development. Tea estates were being managed excellently by British firms and by those few Ceylonese capitalists who had of late been investing in tea. During the war Ceylon had earned a lot of sterling—over a thousand million rupees —which, if managed carefully, could be utilized for the country's economic development. There would be no lack of foreign exchange to undertake and finance long-term developmental projects.

The war had also been a disguised blessing in the matter of the production of food grains in the country. Earlier, the emphasis had been decidedly on cash crops; over 50 per cent of the rice consumed in the country had to be imported. Because of the interruption of the usual sources of supply and the difficulties of overseas trade, a great effort was made during the war to produce rice and other subsidiary crops. The increase in food prices gave added incentive to such activity, which was enthusiastically undertaken in the villages. The new government could make use of this enthusiasm and lend its strong support to this neglected aspect of the country's economy.

There had also been a great improvement in the country's health services during wartime. When Ceylon became the seat of the South-East Asia Command, a large number of troops were stationed in all parts of the country. Thus remote and inaccessible villages received attention they had not had before, and diverse modern amenities were made available to them. Among the most valuable of these was the concentrated fight against malaria, which had been the scourge of the Ceylonese peasant. The success of this campaign was seen in a significant drop in the incidence of this disease by 1947.

Nor was the educational level of the people at the time of independence discouraging. Roughly 60 per cent of the people were literate, if literacy is given its broadest definition. The school system was well organized, and, by an act of 1944, the state undertook the full cost of education in the country. Tuition fees were waived for all students from the kindergarten to the university. Though this was only a part of the costs incurred by a student for his education, it was no doubt a great blessing in a country of low incomes and large families. Teachers in all schools, government and private, were paid by the state.

It thus seemed that the outlook was bright when Ceylon was launched as an independent state in February, 1948. There was every prospect that the democratic tradition would take root and that the country would progress toward material prosperity and contentment. Ceylon seemed to represent the ideal of advance from colonial status to a free nation. A closer look at the scene, however, showed some ominous portents.

It is an important feature of the political scene in Ceylon that its independence was achieved by negotiation and amicable discussions. The conference room and the council chamber were the scenes of activity, in contrast to the public demonstrations and civil disturbances of India. There was no occasion to associate and involve the masses in the struggle and to infuse in them the nationalistic emotion that would encourage them to make sacrifices in the cause of independence. The nationalist parties that were in existence toward the end of British rule spent more of their time fighting each other than fighting the colonial government and therefore did not see the need to enlist the active support of the masses on nationalist issues. Electoral battles of these years were mainly personal affairs fought on parochial lines. None of the parties had grass roots organizations on the village level. One has only to compare the two National Congresses, the Indian and the Ceylonese, to see the way in which the former towered over Indian politics from the date of its formation and the latter competed weakly with numerous other parties and died a natural death when independence was declared.

The manner in which the political negotiations for independence were carried out has given the impression that what happened in February, 1948, was a private transfer of control from colonial rule into the hands of an oligarchy. The power elite at this time consisted of a few families from the dominant sectors of society. No doubt this oligarchy was confirmed in power by popular vote in 1947, but it was still an oligarchy in the sense that no outsiders could get into it. People who held the highest offices were connected by family ties, and the structure of politics resembled somewhat the politics of England under George III.

An even more important drawback arose from the fact that, by the very nature of politics and the political institutions, only the English-educated could aspire to power. Parliamentary government, freedom of the individual, and the whole structure of new ideas were comprehensible to them and them alone. With universal adult suffrage, every individual of the country had been emancipated and brought within the ambit of political power. Yet 95 per cent of the population could not aspire to positions of power because they were not equipped to acquire power and use it. They had been content since 1931, when adult franchise was introduced, to select their leaders from a class which was alien to them. How long they would remain so was another matter. When they comprehended the democratic process and saw to what use they might put it, they would no longer want to rely on the English-educated elite to represent them and manage their affairs.

The westernized elite was not different from the masses only in that they read, wrote, and spoke English. What was more disturbing was the cultural cleavage that separated them from the majority of the people. They had become a separate caste with some of the characteristics that separated traditional castes from each other. Their way of life, their dress, their speech, their cultural interests were different from those of the rest of the country. Most members of this class had uprooted themselves from their traditional milieu and suffered the little that remained to tie them to traditional society like millstones around their necks. Some of them had adopted Western culture and found satisfaction and happiness in it. Others were cultural "mongrels," or, at best, cosmopolitans indecisively trying to fuse aspects of diverse and often conflicting cultures.

Society was thus deeply divided in two: the English-educated and the others. Those not educated in English were condemned to subordinate roles in society. This was satisfactory so long as the mass of the people selected as their leaders members of the westernized oligarchy—who were, after all, better equipped to administer the country's affairs. This is what happened for a decade after independence, and it was found to work well. But it is useful here to recognize the malaise of Ceylon's democracy at the time it was launched and to understand this source of discontent in the subsequent developments of the island's history.

The westernized power elite that took over the leadership of the country was naturally oriented toward the West and looked to Britain for its lead in many matters. Its leaders could describe the island as a "little bit of England" and take pride in this description. British interests continued to dominate the country's economy. A large part of the plantation sector was owned and managed by British companies, as was also a major share of the country's trade and industry. The presence of British armed forces was insured by a defense agreement between the governments of the United Kingdom and Ceylon permitting the British to maintain their forces in Ceylon for its defense. This meant, among other things, that the large airfield at Katunayake and the beautiful natural harbor of Trincomalee continued to be under British control.

If the new leadership felt that it could ignore these factors, it was making a serious miscalculation. It was true that anti-British nationalism had never been born as a mass phenomenon in Ceylon. The absence of mass involvement in nationalist policies was both a cause and a symptom of this factor. Yet the continued physical presence of the British could become a source of irritation to nationalist sentiment. Unless the new government concentrated pressure for the gradual removal of the British, the latter's presence was likely to be used by nationalist politicians as a weapon of attack against the whole new structure. Indeed, there was already a point of view being voiced that the independence granted in 1948 was "fake," that "real" independence could only be won with the removal of the Commonwealth links, as Burma had chosen to do. All British troops should quit the country, and no bases and other facilities should be granted to them. No doubt this was as yet a minority viewpoint and was limited in its circulation. The masses were neither overenthusiastic nor terribly disappointed at the turn of events.

For the successful working of the new constitution, a healthy party system had to develop. This was just beginning, all too shakily. The splinter groups that gathered around influential personalities in the Donoughmore era would not do now. Strong, vigorous political parties with firm and identifiable policies and leadership were required. No doubt the elite, as seen earlier, was familiar with the functioning of the parliamentary system in Britain. But in the actual task of making this system work there were found other difficulties inherent in Ceylonese society. In this respect, the effect of the whole Donoughmore structure had been against the growth of strong parties. Under the executive committee system it had been unnecessary to attach oneself to a political party—in fact it might have been a handicap to do so. The spirit of compromise so essential to the formation of a party had not developed. It was impossible to produce this overnight.

A significant step was taken when the legatees of political power organized themselves into the United National Party (UNP) under the leadership of Mr. D. S. Senanayake. Into this party came members of many groups, communal and otherwise, of the Donoughmore era. Its major constituent units were the Ceylon National Congress, the Sinhala Maha Sabha, and the Muslim League. Most of the other nonparty politicians from all sectors of society decided to join this party also. Being assured of a tenure of political power, it assumed the aspect of a bandwagon. Drawing to it people of diverse political origin, some of whom had no idea that politics had anything to do with principles, this coalition still had to be shaped into a meaningful political grouping. Being the governing party, it had to acquire a political philosophy, a policy, and a sense of disciplined behavior.

Outside the UNP were a number of smaller parties unrelated to each other. On the far left were three Marxist parties—the Lanka Sama Samajist Party (LSSP), the Bolshevik-Leninist Party, and the Communist Party—divided among themselves on both ideological and personal grounds. Quite different from these parties of the left were two communal organizations representing two of the island's minority communities. The Tamil Congress sought to represent those Tamils who had been domiciled in Ceylon for centuries. This party was dissatisfied with the weight given to minorities under the new constitution. Its aim was to unite the Tamils under one flag so that they could put pressure on the Sinhalese and resist any encroachment on their rights. The Ceylon Indian Congress represented the interests of the Tamils who had immigrated to Ceylon within the last hundred years. The bulk of them were plantation workers, from whom the main strength of this party was drawn.

Thus, on the eve of independence there was available a political party to take up the reins of office. But for the efficient working of parliamentary government it is not sufficient that there be a party in office; there should also be a strong party in opposition. The idea of an alternative government is crucial to the British type of representative rule that was being introduced into Ceylon. The distressing factor on the Ceylonese political scene was the absence of such an alternate party wedded to the idea of a democratic alternative to the government in power. The communal parties were all too restricted in their scope and aims to have any effect on a national level. The leftist parties were committed to revolutionary action in diverse forms and would not take the parliamentary scene very seriously. There were a large number of independent politicians not attached to any party, but they were only waiting to make up their minds after they knew which party would form the government. The absence of a national democratic alternative in the first postwar elections of 1947 was a serious drawback in the democratic process. The resultant absence of constructive criticism of government policy was bound to produce an attitude of smugness among governing circles.

The Marxist left, both communist and noncommunist, is an interesting phenomenon of this period. It was a by-product of the study and understanding of Western political thought and institutions that had been introduced under British rule. Its leadership was drawn from the very same English-educated class that produced the ruling oligarchy. Some of these intellectuals had come under the influence of Marxian socialist ideas while studying in British universities. When they returned home they collected a following of young men with left-wing political views. They formed the LSSP in 1935 as a socialist party professing the Marxist approach. When Leon Trotsky was expelled from the Soviet Union after his differences with the Soviet Communists, the Ceylon socialists of the LSSP chose to follow his interpretation of Marxism and become Trotskyite in their orientation. This divided the party into two factions, and with the Nazi-Soviet Pact of 1939 this split was brought to a head. The faction which followed the official Soviet line faithfully through every change and turn broke away to become the Communist Party associated with the Comintern. The LSSP continued as an independent socialist party and developed connections with the Trotskyite Fourth International formed, with its headquarters in Paris, as a rival to the Comintern. In 1945 it divided again when a faction left to form the Bolshevik-Leninist Party. Thus the brief history of the left movement has been dogged by disunity on both theoretical and personal issues. None of these parties was individually of such strength as to challenge the ruling party. Their influence was restricted to urban areas of the western coast and working class concentrations. They lacked the organization and the appeal to expand their activities on a nation-wide basis.

The leftist parties, if they could not provide a constructive alternative to the ruling party, could always be of nuisance value. Their strength and energies were concentrated among the urban working classes. Though these were still a small minority of the total population, their role in the country's economy was an important one. From its inception, the Marxist movement worked among these people and sought to win them over. Workers in industry, commerce, and transport were organized into labor unions under the aegis of one of the three leftist parties. Thus, trade unionism in Ceylon became politically oriented, and this remained an important factor in the development of independent Ceylon. It also meant the introduction of rival unions in the same trade affiliated to different parties of the left. It paved the way for the use of trade union strength for political purposes. The strike of government clerks for full trade union rights in 1947 was an indication of an awareness of this strength. The support of the working classes, including the "white collar" workers, was alienated from the new government and distributed among parties that were wedded to a program of revolutionary action and denial of the constitutional structure. It was an ill omen for the young democracy.

The elections of 1947 resulted in the formation of a government led by Senanayake. Though the party he headed won only 42 seats in a house of 101, with the support of some of the 21 "independent" members elected and the 6 nominated by the Governor, he was able to secure a working majority. On the 4th of February, 1948, the independent constitution was inaugurated by the Duke of Gloucester acting on behalf of the Queen of Great Britain, and Ceylon became a dominion. Thus began a ten-year period of rule by the United National Party. These years are a distinct phase of the island's history and must be discussed separately.

PROBLEMS AND POLITICS, 1947-1962

During this period the democratic process was seen to operate on the three occasions when the island's electors chose their rulers. In 1947 the Senanayake government was installed in power, in 1952 the same party was confirmed in power under the leadership of Senanayake's son Dudley, and in 1956 the party was rejected by the voters in favor of another. This is a notable achievement in the recent history of Ceylon. Because of its compactness and small size, the electorate could give expression successfully to the popular will, and the general elections were in a real sense an expression of this will. The continuing experience of exercising the vote gave even the most remote villager a sense of participation in this democratic process and strengthened his conviction in representative government as an institution relevant to his immediate needs. The governments that held office during these years were thus legitimized by the popular will and governed by popular consent.

Other democratic institutions were also nurtured and built into the political tradition. Parliament grew into an indispensable forum of political debate, respected as such by government and oppositions. As representatives were still drawn from the English-educated, its debates were conducted mainly in English and were of a high standard. Procedure was modeled on the rules of the House of Commons. Under the first Speaker, the efficient Sir Francis Molamure, the House of Representatives developed its own rules for the conduct of business. The opposition produced during this period some debaters of very high caliber, and this fortuitous circumstance induced, especially among the leftist parties, a greater regard for Parliament and a greater preoccupation with their rights within Parliament. Proceedings of

Parliament were widely reported in the press and followed with great interest by the ordinary man. The party system was generally strengthened with experience, and in time parties developed outline policies and programs. In the three elections, the healthy tendency was toward the progressive reduction of those elected as nonparty or independent candidates.

One of the noted developments of this period was the strengthening of the rule of law by an independent and impartial judiciary and an effective administrative machinery. The constitutional provisions protecting both the judiciary and the administration from executive interference were, to a large extent, observed. Because of the defense agreement with Britain it was not necessary to incur the hazards of raising a large armed force. The military consumed less than four per cent of the government budget and, unlike the situation in some other Asian countries, was never in a position to interfere in politics. Public peace was effectively maintained by a civilian police force, and there were judicial safeguards against police excesses. The bureaucracy did not grow to the dimensions it reached in India because of the smallness of the country, but continued to perform its tasks efficiently under political control. There appeared to be a healthy balance among the various institutions of democracy. None of them had the potential of menacing the growing democratic tradition.

An important feature in all this was the father figure of D. S. Senanayake, who dominated the first five years of this period. Though not himself highly educated, he belonged to a family which had adopted Western culture rather early. The oldest of the politicians of the time, and one who had led the negotiations for independence, he very soon filled the position of an elder statesman. Circumstances and deliberate propaganda built him into the father of the Nation. Though he had none of the charismatic qualities of a Nehru, he was the closest approximation Ceylon had of such a personality. He was the symbol of the country's unity because he soon won the confidence of the Tamils, the largest minority, both by his excellent personal relations and by his wise political stratagems. He was also able to dominate the Cabinet, which was fortunate, since the Cabinet was more a coalition of diverse forces than a single homogenous entity. He was able to settle disputes between quarrelsome ministers and weld a hastily collected group of individualistic politicians into a party with some central theme. He achieved a great success and strengthened his government when he won over the Tamil Congress and brought its leader into the Cabinet. Senanayake's value to the country and to his party was demonstrated upon his sudden death in March, 1952. There was no obvious successor. After a brief period of hesitant leadership by Senanayake's son, Sir John Kotelawala became prime minister and leader of the party from October, 1953, until its electoral demise of 1956. The UNP never really recovered from the loss of its founder.

Corresponding to this entrenchment of democratic institutions within the country was the establishment of prestige and reputation abroad, especially among the Western powers. The three UNP administrations of this period were in no doubt where the interests of the country lay in its external relations. The first government had signed the agreements with the British government on defense and external affairs, both of which were of importance in her foreign policy. By the agreement on defense she entrusted the defense of the country to Britain's imperial forces. The agreement on external affairs provided for consultations between the foreign offices of Britain and Ceylon and insured that the inexperienced Ceylonese officials would be supplied with information from British sources. It also provided for Ceylon's representation in countries where she did not have her own mission by the representatives of the United Kingdom. These agreements remained the keystone of Ceylon's foreign policy until 1956, and succeeding UNP administrations stood by this Anglo-Ceylonese alliance steadfastly in the face of mounting domestic opposition.

Following from this basic position, there was also no doubt regarding Ceylon's stand in the international politics of the growing Cold War. She was decidedly friendly to the Western bloc, though none of her governments would commit her decisively to any one of the Western-led military alliances in the region. The third prime minister, Kotelawala, was very anxious to take Ceylon into SEATO but desisted, deferring to a climate in the country hostile to such action. That Soviet Russia too was in no doubt of Ceylon's attitude can be seen in her repeated vetoes of Ceylon's application to the United Nations. She was finally admitted only in 1955 as part of a package deal between the communists and the West. All three prime ministers were outspoken in their attack on communism and the communist states. Kotelawala went furthest in this respect. He incurred the wrath of the neutralist states in the Bandung Conference of Asian countries by seeking to get them to condemn communist imperialism along with their condemnation of the Western brand. An influential group within the government was anxious that ties as friendly as those with the British be developed with the United States. They recognized the growing importance of America in the postwar world, together with the fact that Britain was declining to the position of a second- or third-rate power. But they had to move cautiously lest they expose themselves to attack by nationalist and communist-inspired forces. "Wall Street imperialism" was just beginning to become an effective emotional concept in the political scene. Even within the governing circle there were some who had been caught up in this incipient anti-Americanism. As to the British connection, there was unanimity in its favor.

A significant breach was made in the anticommunist foreign policy when a rubber-rice trade agreement was concluded in 1952 with Communist China. The falling prices for rubber in the world market led Ceylon to tap other sources. China was in need of this strategic commodity and made price offers substantially higher than the prevailing market price. The year was a bad one for rice, too, which China offered to sell. Hence a barter agreement was made by which China bought a certain quantity of rubber and sold to Ceylon a certain quantity of rice at fixed prices. This caused a change in the pattern of Ceylon's trade. Though it did not result in a softening of the anticommunist approach of the government, it did show a greater independence from Western pressure. The unfortunate attempts by the United States government to block this agreement hastened the spread of anti-American feelings among the educated middle class.

During this period Ceylon was the beneficiary of foreign aid initiated by the Western democracies. This was the result both of the comparatively successful working of the democratic machinery in Ceylon and of the generally pro-Western policies of its government. The most important of these schemes was the Colombo Plan. Initiated by the Commonwealth countries, the consultations in 1950-51 resulted in the establishment of a Colombo Plan organization. It was expanded to include underdeveloped Asian countries outside the Commonwealth. Through this scheme, Ceylon was the recipient of considerable capital assistance and technical know-how. An American aid agreement was concluded in 1956, one of the last acts of the UNP government. By this Ceylon received food grains and technical assistance of diverse forms.

However much the government was by its inclination and self-interest oriented toward the West, it could not overlook the fact that, as a newly independent Asian country, it had certain responsibilities toward its Asian neighbors. It attempted to play a part in the growing solidarity of Asia, though not always with conviction. In 1949, when the Dutch attempted to suppress the Indonesian nationalist revolution, the UNP government of Ceylon prohibited the use of its harbor and airport to the Dutch for transporting military personnel. This was a very popular move in Ceylon and, indeed, throughout Asia.

In the development of Asian solidarity, relations with India were crucial. Here there was a divergence of approach between the two governments up to 1956. Ceylon was confessedly depending on the West for its defense and had offered bases to the British. India had fashioned a policy which sought by nonalignment to remove India and, if possible, her neighbouring territories from the theater of the Cold War conflict. Correspondingly, Ceylon was anticommunist, while India was at this time refusing to become involved in any crusade against communism. This divergence was pointed up in the Colombo Conference of 1954 and the Bandung Conference of 1955. At the Colombo Conference, India, Pakistan, Burma, and Indonesia were the guests of Ceylon. Kotelawala attempted to persuade these powers to condemn communism as an even greater threat to the new Asian countries than Western imperialism. This was opposed by Nehru, and finally a compromise formula was agreed upon which condemned communist and colonial intervention in the internal affairs of independent countries. At the Bandung Conference of 1955 the conflict was even sharper. This was a conference of all Asian countries, to whom India's chief aim was to present China as a respectable power in international politics. Here too, Kotelawala brought up the subject of the new colonialism, to Nehru's great exasperation. The difference on military agreements with Western powers also came up at the conference. In all these matters Ceylon showed herself closer to Pakistan than to India in her attitudes.

The presence of a sizable minority of Indian immigrants on the island further vitiated relations between the two countries. These immigrants numbered about 800,000, the bulk of whom were descendants of indentured laborers brought from India to work on the plantations. The liberal franchise rules at the time of independence gave them all the vote, and their concentration at the center of the island enabled them to send seven representatives to the first Parliament. By the Indian and Pakistani Citizenship Act of 1949, the UNP government formulated its definition of citizenship rights. The result was to disenfranchise the entire lot and create difficulties with the Indian government. India refused to accept them as her citizens, and thus a community of "stateless" people came into existence. Periodic negotiations between the two governments on the question of how many of these could be absorbed by Ceylon and on what basis proved fruitless. This unresolved issue stood in the way of close relations between the two countries and, indeed, produced a general anti-Indian sentiment among certain sections of the population, a feeling which was shrewdly exploited by politicians.

Although there was no coordinated plan of economic development during this period, some significant advances were made in particular fields. The large sterling balance accumulated during the war and reasonably good terms of trade, at least for the first five years, made possible large outlays of capital on major development works. All governments of this period were eager to expand the agricultural sector of the economy. The pressure of population in the western and southern coastal regions and the necessity to import large quantities of rice resulted in the preoccupation of governments with agrarian and land policies. It was in the dry zone of Ceylon, once the home of flourishing rice cultivation, that expansion of production could be sought. By reconstructing and widening old irrigation works and clearing jungle, new land could be reclaimed where the landless farmers of other regions could be settled with state assistance. This had already been started years before independence, and the new government vigorously extended the policy.

A large amount of capital was sunk into these colonization schemes. The reservoirs were extended at great cost. Settlers were provided with a house and monthly allowances to tide them over the initial period. The amount of land available ranged from eight acres at the beginning to four acres at the later stages. Selected colonists had to be landless farmers with large families. To prevent fragmentation, the curse of the Ceylonese peasant, land could be inherited by only one of the descendants. The government ran a whole gamut of services to look after the interests of the colonists. Cooperative societies guaranteed the sales of their produce at specific prices, although very soon illegal middlemen sprang up and deprived the peasant of a considerable revenue. The adoption of scientific techniques of farming increased yields and promoted efficient land use. The biggest of these schemes was a multipurpose project on the bed of the Gal Oya river in east Ceylon, embracing land settlement, hydroelectric power, cotton and sugar plantations, and small industries. It was run by a statutory board, independent and self-sufficient, managing all affairs in that extensive valley.

Tea and rubber, and, to a lesser degree, coconut, continued to be the firm props of the country's economy. Tea production was largely European-owned; it flourished in the background of government friendship toward British enterprise and was the biggest earner of foreign exchange. Rubber fluctuated more than tea, and the market in this period was not at all steady. The Korean war gave a temporary boom to this industry, and with the end of the Korean war came the five-year rubber-rice agreement with China. With stable prices ensured, the government was able to undertake replanting and rehabilitation of this industry. Further attempts at development included nascent secondary industries. Among the factories set up by the government were those for the manufacture of paper, caustic soda, and cement. Other capital ventures of this period were the extension of the Colombo harbor and a hydro-electric scheme at Norton Bridge.

Behind this façade of democratic development and economic prosperity many problems lay hidden. Fundamentally, many of these problems had economic origins, though they manifested themselves in various other forms. The government's attempts to deal with the country's economic problems lacked method and vigor. It had inherited an economy which was superficially sound but lopsided. The government had in its hands the means with which to mend this lopsidedness, but, because everything was going satisfactorily at the beginning of independence—and, indeed, the government had come to power in a wave of prosperity—it assumed that things would continue in this fashion. And when, in the Fifties, the economy had to suffer the ups and downs of world trends, the government was not prepared to face this situation. Both the politicians and their economic advisers were wedded to laissez-faire economic theories. They expected the open-door policy to lead to a significant influx of foreign capital, but this did not take place. The liberal tariff policy of the period resulted in an influx of luxury goods, temporarily benefiting the affluent classes, whose spending spree wasted considerable reserves of foreign assets the country had built up.

The absence of a definite plan, or at least some well-defined goals, was a great handicap. There was no central, knowledgeable organization to consider how the country's limited resources might best be utilized and to give final judgment of priorities on schemes brought forth by various ministers. Only in the twilight of its power did the last UNP government seek to establish a planning secretariat, which produced a six-year program of investment. Thus, schemes tended to be considered and adopted on account of some immediate advantages or from political considerations, rather than on their long-term benefit to the country.

After the death of the first prime minister in 1952, economic problems came to a head. Terms of world trade were turning to Ceylon's disadvantage. Social and welfare services in the country consumed around 35 per cent of the budget, and the country was feeling the strain. Extended health and welfare benefits had resulted in a phenomenal 2.8 per cent growth of population. A World Bank mission which studied the economy in 1952 drew attention to this incongruity of accelerated population growth and lagging productivity. The seriousness of the foreign exchange position made the economic advisers look around for a likely retrenchment on social services. They recommended that the government subsidy on rice, which accounted for a great proportion of this expenditure, be reduced. When Prime Minister Dudley Senanayake accepted this advice and increased the consumer's price of rice, he was faced with a hue and cry throughout the country. A civil disobedience movement led to violence and government reprisals and resulted in the prime minister's resignation. Under the last UNP government all the subsidies on education, food, and welfare imposed a growing strain on a stagnant economy. It was politically dangerous to curtail any of these benefits, and the government was in a quandary.

There were other aspects as well in which an apparent calm merely hid smoldering issues from view. It has been stated earlier in this chapter that power in Ceylon was transferred from the colonial government to the westernized elite, and that the latter was but a tiny minority of the population. This state of affairs could not last long in an independent democratic country. The wisest course for the leadership would have been to institute a gradual introduction of members of the non-Western intelligentsia to positions of political power. Instead, very little was done toward this end. The language of administration, even where it came directly into touch with the people, was still English, as in the colonial days. Educational policy and its results showed the incongruities inherent in this situation. There were schools teaching in English and schools teaching in Sinhalese and Tamil. The latter were, however, very much the poor relations. English schools were better equipped and their teachers better paid, and their graduates could aspire to a university education. Sinhalese- and Tamil-educated pupils had to end their education at the level of the School Certificate. Some could enter teachers' training colleges. For the others, the only employment their education made possible was in the lowest grades of public administration. Thus, an English school product with the School Certificate could become a clerk in government service and thereafter rise to the highest positions. A Sinhalese school youth with the same certificate had to work as a subordinate all his life. In 1951 the government sought to redeem this anomaly by introducing compulsory study of the mother tongue at the secondary school level. But the remedy was to some extent worse than the disease, and this switchover without adequate preparation played havoc with the educational system.

As the English-educated elite further entrenched their position under UNP rule, they became the focus of the opposition of people outside the ruling group, an opposition based on economic considerations—the lack of opportunity to improve their lot. The Sinhalese-educated population were in a position of impoverishment largely because they could not influence the policies of the government. Their participation in two postwar general elections, besides a number of local elections, gave them an awareness of their power in a democracy. If only they could be better organized and more articulate, if they could form pressure groups and participate in organized political activity, then they could have a greater influence on the country's politics. Potential groups that might wield influence were associations of Sinhalese teachers, of Ayurvedic* physicians, and of village headmen. For the greater part of the duration of UNP rule, these groups had no unity of purpose, and their strength was dissipated in several splinter societies. They had no training in organized leadership or disciplined activity. But, goaded by the impact of UNP policies and by years of neglect, they were bestirring themselves. Toward the end of the period of UNP rule they had grouped themselves more rationally and were getting a clearer perspective on their true interests.

This politico-economic problem was intertwined with a religious and cultural one. The history of Buddhism in Ceylon, its introduction and spread, its schisms, its glory and decline, have given the island, or at least the Sinhalese people, a unifying thread connecting the present with the past. In the period of the classical Sinhalese kingdoms there had been a close affinity between the state and the Buddhist faith. Its priesthood, though monastic in character, had developed traditions of laboring in society and wielding influence in its day-to-day activities. During colonial rule, Buddhist influence on state and society naturally suffered a setback. Christianity was the favored religion and attracted to it the loyalties of some Sinhalese and Tamils. Favorable government policies, private missionary assistance from the West, and most particularly their control of educational in-

* A form of indigenous medicine.

stitutions enabled the minority Christian communities to rise to a dominant position in society. In the absence of state support, Buddhism declined and at the time of independence showed the ill-effects of this unequal competition.

A revivalist movement had begun in the last decades of the nineteenth century, under the delayed influence of the Hindu reformation movements of India. But it did not have that organic link with nationalism that it had in India where, under Ghandhi, Hindu values were increasingly stressed and nationalism given a religious base. With independence it was necessary to stress Ceylon's distinctiveness. The "a little bit of England" attitude was all right for the westernized middle class. It would not do for the great mass of the Sinhalese people, for whom an emphasis on Buddhism, its past glories and the importance of its values for the future, was a key to achieve such distinctiveness. In the best tradition of British liberalism, the UNP leaders sought to maintain the state as a secular institution that did not interfere in the affairs of the various religions whether to the advantage or disadvantage of these religions. UNP rule was a period of religious peace and harmony in the island because the government chose not to disturb the *status quo*. While this is a commendable attitude in a country where different religions have secured an equilibrium of power and influence, it is not so when there are religious groups harboring grievances, both real and imaginary, and thinking that the time has come to redress these grievances. Even the UNP found that they had to cater to Buddhist feelings during elections, especially in view of the growing Marxist challenge. The 2,500th anniversary of the death of the Buddha, coinciding in Sinhalese tradition with the landing of the first Sinhalese prince, Vijaya, and his followers in Ceylon, combined to make the year 1956 a singular one. The celebrations infused a sense of pride in Buddhist religion and history.

In the view of the more dogmatic Buddhists, the country was being impregnated under UNP rule with an alien culture and alien values that would undermine and destroy traditional culture. For them independence had not only to be a liberation from Western rule, it had also to be accompanied by a repudiation of everything that the Westerner had brought. It meant going back to the roots of its traditions and thus enriching the nation. The past was presented as one of glory and prosperity and, what is more, everything in that past was held to be relevant to the Sinhalese of the present. The Buddha Jayanti Year was the occasion for incursions into the past in the press and on the platform, and Ceylon's history was treated in such a way that the four centuries of Western rule did not and ought not to count. In what may be termed this second phase of Buddhist revivalism, the Western-educated Buddhist, the non-Western intelligentsia, and the humble peasant all participated.

There were thus economic, religious, and cultural factors of discontent with UNP rule. But these did not become issues of politics for some time. Politics was still the monopoly of the English-educated, and only when such causes could find support among this elite could they be raised to the arena of national politics. In this respect, the defection of Mr. S. W. R. D. Bandaranayake from the UNP in 1951 is an important watershed in the political history of Ceylon.

Bandaranayake came from a family of highly westernized Sinhalese Christians who had held positions of authority under British rule. He himself had his early education in an Anglican public school in Colombo and proceeded to Oxford, where he took a degree and later qualified as a barrister in one of the Inns of Court. Yet, instead of absorbing such westernizing influences, he rejected many of the Western elements of his background. He embraced the Buddhist faith, affected national modes of dress (then very unpopular among members of his class), and upheld nationalist political causes. In 1937 he formed the Sinhala Maha Sabha as a movement within the National Congress, with similar objectives but with a stress on the particular interests of the Sinhalese in political affairs. This was the only wing of the nationalist movement that sought to reach the Sinhalese population and to infuse a Sinhala-consciousness within a Ceylonese nationalism. Thus, very early in life Bandaranayake showed an inkling of his subsequent political development.

When the UNP was formed with the Sinhala Maha Sabha as a constituent unit, Bandaranayake became a prominent member of the Cabinet and minister of local government and health. He maintained intact the Sabha and its organization, which served him as a useful platform to retain his connections with his followers. He would now and again use this platform to criticize UNP policies, a strategy which retarded the growth of the governing coalition into a cohesive and well-knit party and caused embarrassment to the prime minister. Finally, in 1951 he decided to part company with the UNP, resigned his office, crossed the floor, and announced the formation of a new party, the Sri Lanka Freedom Party (SLFP). This was a landmark in the growth of parliamentary democracy in Ceylon. Here was a national party wedded to the democratic structure offering itself as an alternative to the UNP. People now had a third choice which lay between the policies of the UNP and the revolutionary socialism of the Marxist left.

Bandaranayake's dissatisfaction arose from UNP's failure to bridge the gap between the Sinhalese-educated population and the westernized elite. Even while in office as a Cabinet minister, he had championed the cause of various Sinhalese professional organizations. He felt that insufficient attention was paid to traditional Sinhalese culture and Buddhist values, that these should find a greater place in state policies. His economic policies were mildly socialistic, and he disagreed with the emphasis on free enterprise. He felt that the state should play a greater role in bringing about an egalitarian society. The policies of the new party were thus meant to absorb the discontented Sinhalese and to champion their interests. The new emphasis on nationalism was intended to bring the Sinhalese into a consciousness of their nationhood that would not be limited to a hybrid Ceylonese concept, which he dismissed as Western and middle class. The Sinhala nation were to come forward from the villages to assert themselves and wrest power from the English-educated, urban elite, who were antinational in outlook. The Sinhalese language and the Buddhist religion were to be raised in status. In the first elections the party contested in 1952 it did not fare well. It still lacked nation-wide organization and funds, and out of 48 seats contested it won but 9. Nevertheless, Bandaranayake was elected leader of the opposition.

The Marxist left was not a serious parliamentary threat to the UNP. It continued to be disunited throughout the period of UNP rule, and efforts at unity only ended in greater disunity. Electorally the Marxist parties fared worse than the SLFP in 1952, and their seats were reduced from 20 to 13. The appearance of the SLFP affected their fortunes adversely, because whatever votes they had attracted on a purely anti-UNP basis were now shared with the SLFP. In the rural areas, the policies of the SLFP appealed far more and were more comprehensible than Marxist theories of social revolution. Since they lacked parliamentary influence, these parties sought to exert influence through extraparliamentary means. By their hold on trade unions they promoted strikes. The one major instance of their organized opposition to government was the *hartal*, or civil disobedience movement, of August, 1953, to protest the withdrawal of the subsidy on rice. This showed that the leftist parties could bring down governments even if they could not form them.

In the last years of UNP rule, these oppositions marshaled their forces. The 1956 election was a turning point in the history of Ceylon and well-nigh produced a social revolution. It resulted in the dethronement of the westernized elite, both professional and commercial, which had dominated the politics of Ceylon for over 25 years. In their place it enthroned the nationalist-minded elite and the Sinhalese-educated professional classes. It thus broadened the base of political power and in a sense made Ceylon's democracy more genuinely democratic. It altered the nature and content of politics and introduced new values and even a new terminology to the political scene.

It is important to look into the issues that dominated the election struggle of 1955-56 if we are to understand the course of politics in the postelection years. One factor that distinguished this election from the previous ones is that the voters this time had a more meaningful choice. Bandaranayake, in preparation for the election, formed a coalition with a few other minor parties and called it the Mahajana Eksath Peramune (Peoples' United Front—MEP). The SLFP was the dominant partner of this coalition. Second in importance was one of the three Marxist parties, led by Mr. Philip Goonewardena, besides which there came into the alliance a few of those *ad hoc* political groups that usually surface before a general election. The MEP put up 60 candidates and offered itself as a party that could form an alternative government. Hence votes given against the UNP government were not just protest votes which would have no value in the formation of a government. What is more, the SLFP had further fortified itself by a no-contest agreement with the Marxist parties. This again meant that the voter was, in a majority of constituencies, given a straight choice between two candidates, in contrast to lengthy lists of candidates in previous elections.

The MEP fought the elections on a bold language-religion-culture front. Language especially was coming to the fore as a live issue from 1955 onward. A subtle twist given to this issue served the immediate political needs of the party. The feeling that the languages spoken by the majority of the people must be developed and raised to the level of the English language was as old as nationalism itself. Up to this time, when politicians talked of a changeover in the official language from English, they assumed that its place would be taken by both major indigenous languages. Now the MEP asserted that only Sinhalese would be given official status and, overnight, for the ordinary Sinhalese the enemy became not merely English but Tamil as well. Thus the UNP was chided not only for not recognizing the Sinhalese language but also for seeking to give equality of status to Tamil. The fight for recognition of the Sinhalese language was telescoped with the need to remove from Tamil the status of a national language.

Everyone who talked of making both Sinhalese and Tamil official now became the enemy of the Sinhalese. Here the leftists were affected adversely. Based on economic and political ideologies with nation-wide appeal, they had written into their programs that English should be replaced by Sinhalese and Tamil. These parties, both the Communist Party and the LSSP, had now to share the opprobrium of being "friends of the Tamils." The popular slogan of the election was not just "Sinhala" but "Sinhala-only." The UNP sought belatedly to ride on the crest of this wave and changed its language policy to "Sinhala-only" as well. But this dishonorable maneuver only cost it the support of the Tamils without regaining the confidence of the Sinhalese.

Second to language came the cry of "Buddhism in danger." The alleged sources of the danger were the policies of the UNP and the conspiracy of the Roman Catholic Church. SLFP propaganda conjured up an anti-Buddhist front of the UNP and the Church. Some credence was given to this otherwise ridiculous allegation by the ill-advised interference by some Catholic prelates in this and previous elections on behalf of the UNP. An important tool for this propaganda was the report of the Buddhist commission set up by an influential body of Buddhist laymen, the All-Ceylon Buddhist Congress, in 1954 to report on the state of Buddhism in Ceylon. The report, hurriedly drafted and published before the elections, was a formidable analysis of the island's recent history from a highly partisan Buddhist viewpoint. It contained a series of recommendations which, by active state interference, sought to introduce various reforms in the institutions of Buddhism. Both through the Sinhalese press and by cheap Sinhalese editions of the report, these views and remedies became widely known and accepted among the Sinhalese intelligentsia. The SLFP accepted the report and undertook to implement it if elected to power. This brought a solid bloc of Buddhist support, lay and clerical, to the party. Many Buddhist priests, especially in the small village temples, came out electioneering for the party. They were a factor in politics which had not been influential before, or, if at all, only at a personal level.

These issues, which identified certain minorities as enemies of the Sinhalese Buddhists, were dangerously emotional in character. They were issues on which the extremist and the unscrupulous could pour out venom and incite hatred against a section of his compatriots. They could be addressed only to the majority community. The SLFP did not, and indeed could not, put forward candidates in any of the Tamil-speaking electorates. The UNP, after it adopted its "Sinhala-only" program, did not have any candidates in these areas either. The Tamils put forward their own candidates, who differed according to the means by which they would resist the imposition of the Sinhalese language. The Federal Party, with a scheme of a federal constitution, was the chief contender for the Tamil vote. Thus, electoral politics became divided rigidly on communal lines. The only truly national parties were the Marxist parties, which had no chance of being elected to power.

Economic issues were present, though not dominant. Naturally, they were stressed more by the leftist parties. The rice subsidy was of special significance, and, though the increase in the price of rice had been effected in 1953, anti-UNP propagandists saw to it that it was fresh in the people's minds. So also was the withdrawal of a free snack to all school children. General economic distress, unemployment, and underemployment were factors that favored opposition parties. The Marxist parties laid great emphasis on these factors, with a view to distracting the people from emotional issues like language and religion which would have worked against them. These parties, especially the LSSP, offered a comprehensive program of doctrinaire socialism, with nationalization, leveling of incomes by taxation, and a high degree of state planning and development. Insofar as the SLFP paid attention to economic issues, it drew chunks out of the leftist program and pointed to its alliance with one of the leftist parties to prove its socialism and concern for the masses. It is clear, however, that in the avalanche of emotion released by the cultural issues, economic considerations were of marginal effect.

The victory of the MEP and the left over the UNP was decisive but was to some extent a Pyrrhic victory. It was won at the cost of rousing hopes and aspirations in the majority community, the fulfillment of which would severely strain the nation's unity and even undermine its economic foundations. Thus the government that was inaugurated in May, 1956, itself suffered from certain initial handicaps.

The MEP was not a party but a coalition of parties hastily brought together for the purpose of presenting an alternate government to the voter. In this mixed bag of politicians and parties two or three broad strands are identifiable. The core of the party was the SLFP grouped around Bandaranayake and led by him. His policy may be described as one of associating the people more closely with the democratic structure of the country. The Sinhalese Buddhists being the majority, he felt that their interests should predominate, but he had enough of the liberal tradition in him to concede that such dominance does not involve the active suppression of minority interests. Economics was his weak point; apart from a vague egalitarian concept, he had no real concept of the goal or means of his economic program. This was dangerous, because he had been elected on a promise to change the existing structure, and any reformer must first define his aims. On one fringe of his coalition were politicians whose politics consisted of an extreme racialism, a view that the interests of minority communities must be crushed on the road to Sinhalese hegemony. Such politics, which in the UNP era would have been considered as bordering on lunacy, were now made respectable and indeed operated near the seats of power. The left arm of the MEP coalition was the Marxist splinter party of Philip Goonewardena which had two of its leaders in the new Cabinet. They had the merit of a clear idea of economic policy and a clear view of the role of the state in economic development and welfare policies. As minister of agriculture and minister of industries, they held key positions in the government. This lack of cohesion in Cabinet and party dogged the government during its existence. In the event, it was the Marxist tail that wagged the MEP dog.

The new government undertook, soon after its election, to translate into action its promises of giving improved status to the Sinhalese language and the Buddhist religion. A ministry of culture was set up to direct and subvent this revivalist activity. An advisory council appointed to assist the ministry suitably consisted of members of the new elite—Buddhist clergy and Sinhalese pundits. A bill making Sinhalese the official language in place of English was hurriedly drafted and presented to Parliament in June, 1956. An official commission was set up in February, 1957, to report on the manner of implementing the unofficial Buddhist report.

In some of these matters the government was confronted by serious opposition. The "Sinhala-only" legislation, as it came to be known, was the beginning of a tragic history of Sinhalese-Tamil ill feeling in the country. The Tamils, led now by the Federal party, felt that the Tamil language should be recognized equally as an official language. When the bill became law, they began extraparliamentary agitation which fanned the hatred of the Sinhalese toward the Tamils that had been aroused during the elections. The Tamils were unanimous in their demands that, at least in the northern and eastern provinces, where they were concentrated, the language of the Tamils should be the language of administration. Sinhalese extremists in Bandaranayake's coalition would brook of no change in the Language Act, which declared Sinhalese the sole official language throughout the country. They threatened extraparliamentary agitation against any kind of recognition of Tamil. Bandaranayake was thus trapped in the vagueness of his own promises and became the prisoner of the extremists on his side. Every move he made to meet Tamil demands halfway was obstructed by the extremist threat of rousing the Sinhalese people. It was in this context of communal bitterness that the ugly clashes of May and June of 1958 took place, necessitating an extensive transfer of population from both sides of the communal frontier and leaving a deep scar on intercommunal relations in the island.

The plan to rehabilitate Buddhism also met with opposition, now from disagreement regarding method. The fanatics wanted the state to become theocratic, declare Buddhism the official state religion, and subordinate state policies to religious dogma. The more enlightened Buddhists did not wish to go so far and, though they would be free to interfere with affairs of state, did not want the state to interfere with religious affairs. This would, and did, obstruct the functioning of the commission on Buddhism. Generally, the clergy, who aspired to a position of influence in the state were disappointed within two or three years at their share of political power. They distrusted the liberalism of Bandaranayake and his attempts at tolerance toward the minorities. They were impatient with the slow pace of change toward the equalization of opportunities enjoyed by the English-educated and the Sinhalese-educated populations. They were dissatisfied with what was done to strengthen Ayurveda. By 1959 the unity and enthusiasm among the clergy for the new government had evaporated and in certain circles turned to hostility.

The legislative activity of the government in economic matters showed the influence of its left-wing members. Two major steps were taken in the sphere of nationalization of the economy. The omnibus transport services all over the island were nationalized and run by the Ceylon Transport Board. This was a healthy step, eliminating wasteful and unnecessary competition among private companies and enabling the introduction of a nationally planned system of transport throughout the island. Next came the nationalization of the port of Colombo. The Port Cargo Corporation was set up to take charge of all activities there. It reorganized the structure of the port and unified the various services which had heretofore been run by private companies. There was also a greater amount of state activity in the exploration of new avenues of industry. In these new ventures the assistance of communist countries was sought and secured. A cotton spinning mill was set up with Chinese assistance. The government tried to revitalize the cooperative movement by granting monopolies over certain sectors of the import trade. The general policy was to discourage the private entrepreneur and expand the state's functions in every sphere.

In agricultural affairs, this was the first postwar government to attempt seriously the task of land reform. Earlier UNP governments had sought to divert the landless to the uncultivated wastes which it opened up for their benefit. It had tampered on the surface of the problem of feudal relations in land. The Marxist minister of agriculture set about tackling this problem with his customary drive. The Paddy Lands Act of 1958 sought to provide security of tenure to the tenant and curtailed the rights of the landlord over him. The election by tenants of cultivation committees in every locality assured the influence of the tenants over the various technical problems of agriculture and irrigation. Enlightened measures were initiated for insuring the peasant's crop against a bad harvest and thus saving him from the clutches of rural moneylenders. The minister eventually proposed further measures securing rural credit for the peasant and insuring the peasant against indebtedness. But his reforms had trod on too many vested interests with influence in the governing party and Cabinet. Other members of Cabinet were restive at the inevitable growth in his stature and power and suspected him of trying to build political support in the country to promote the sectarian interests of his own party. In 1959, a new scheme by the minister of agriculture for creating rural credit was made the occasion by his colleagues for a showdown, and he and his partymate, the minister of industries, were forced to resign. Their resignation weakened the government and robbed it of whatever left-wing support it had had.

The major failing of the Bandaranayake government was in its role of custodian of law and order in the country. No doubt the government succeeded in awakening the self-consciousness of the Sinhalese and infusing in them a sense of participation in government, but they did not succeed in imparting an awareness of the limitations and obligations of the citizen in a democracy. The lower middle classes and the urban workers who felt a proprietory right to government as a result of the defeat of the UNP in 1956 asserted themselves in ways which were embarrassing to the new government. The absence of strong leadership at the top allowed these diverse pressure groups to get out of hand. Thus, new pressure groups took the place of the old ones that had flourished under the UNP, with the difference that the new men lacked the discretion that comes with experience in politics. Sit-down strikes, *satyagrahas*,* and fasts-unto-death became frequent means of political action, and the government's initial reluctance to assert the executive authority of the state allowed them to flourish. Trade unions, relying on the support of the Marxist wing of government, often resorted to industrial action. The efficient police force was demoralized and depleted by political interference. This weakening of the regular channels for enforcement of authority was partly responsible for the violence of the communal clashes and the necessity to call in the armed forces and resort to emergency regulations.

The Bandaranayake government effected a major change in Ceylon's foreign policy and attitude toward international politics. The prime minister had campaigned against the military agreement with Britain and the concession of bases to British forces. One of his first acts in foreign relations was to negotiate the return of British bases in the island. This was concluded in 1957, and the naval base at Trincomalee and military airport at Katunayake were taken over by the Ceylonese government.

In its general approach to international relations the new government moved closer to the position taken by India. It established closer diplomatic relations with communist countries. There was a perceptible increase in the number of communist diplomatic representatives in Ceylon and in their activities. Cultural missions and dance troupes were exchanged with these countries. Together with other neutralist Asian nations, Ceylon voiced its condemnation of Anglo-French action in Egypt and equivocated over Russian action in Hungary. Western powers continued to be friendly with Ceylon in appreciation of her democratic institutions. American aid, which had begun during UNP rule, was continued and expanded. The Ceylon

* Passive resistance.

delegate at the UN worked more closely with the Afro-Asian group. This, however, did not mean that all differences with India were settled or that Sinhalese suspicions of India were removed. The problem of the Indians in Ceylon could not be settled by Bandaranayake in spite of his ideological proximity to Nehru. They continued as a "stateless" people, denied the rights and privileges of Ceylonese citizens and refused recognition by the Indian government as Indian citizens.

Bandaranayake was fond of referring to his years as prime minister as a period of transition. He would dismiss criticisms of the unrest and turmoil that characterized his period of office as necessary and temporary inconveniences in a time of great changes. There is no doubt that the period was one of change, but it is questionable whether all these changes were beneficial and whether he himself knew and mastered the direction in which the country was changing. Bandaranayake was excellent at destroying the old order with its inequalities and vested interests. But he was less successful in the more formidable task of setting up a meaningful structure in its place, at giving concrete shape to the ideals of democratic nationalism and social equality that he had so eloquently held up before his supporters. His greatest success was in a forceful assertion of Sinhalese and Buddhist rights and in remedying an undoubted injustice that had been done to these people under centuries of colonial rule. But this was achieved at the cost of dividing the nation and causing linguistic and religious grievances among minority groups. Perhaps, left to himself, he might have seen a way to reconcile the predominance of majority interests with the protection of minority rights. But he himself had made these matters issues of politics, and the whole nation was looking over his shoulder and watching his every move.

A group of discontented supporters, drawn from his own party, conspired to assassinate him. The assassin was a *bhikkhu* (monk), whose garb gave him easy access to the prime minister. He performed the act on the 25th of September, 1959; the following day the prime minister died.

This was the tragic climax to a period of violence and lawlessness that had been unleashed by the MEP electoral victory of 1956. It put the governing party in disarray, for the person of Bandaranayake had been the only factor that held the party together. There followed a period of uncertain rule under W. Dhahanayake, a minister of the Bandaranayake Cabinet and member of the SLFP. Defections from the governing party caused by uncertainty about its future prospects made its majority in Parliament very shaky, and the new prime minister decided to go to the country for a mandate in March, 1960. The UNP, heartened by the troubles within the SLFP, made a determined bid to turn to its advantage the widespread disillusion with the government. In the elections it emerged as the largest single party in Parliament, though without an absolute majority. The SLFP came in close behind as the second-largest party. Almost all Tamil seats were won by the Federal Party, which thus confirmed its leadership of the Tamil community. The UNP leader, Dudley Senanayake, was called upon to form a government. A minority government, it did not have the support of any other group in Parliament. The left was strongly opposed to it and was determined to bring it down. It did not get the support of the strong Tamil minority group because it hedged on the subject of concessions on language rights of the Tamils. Senanayake decided to appeal to the country again for a stronger mandate, and a general election was fixed for July, 1960.

The return of the UNP to power and the prospect of its continued exercise of power brought together forces which were united only in their opposition to the UNP. That common aim led to an electoral agreement among these parties similar to the agreement contracted with great success by Bandaranayake before the 1956 elections. The SLFP which fought the July elections was very different from the SLFP which had fought the elections of March. It had been heartened by its performance in March, when it fought against heavy odds and had not yet found a leader to replace the loss of its founder. The March elections had shown that its support among the rural Sinhalese voters was still substantially intact. Suspicion of the UNP as a party inimical to Sinhalese nationalism had not been rooted out. The SLFP's achievement of making Sinhalese the only official language was something the voter could never forget and was never allowed to forget.

Perhaps the most favorable factor of all for the SLFP was

the emergence of Mrs. Sirimavo Bandaranayake, the widow of S. W. R. D. Bandaranayake, to the forefront of politics. Her decision to accept the leadership of the party founded by her late husband was a momentous one, resulting in a massive emotional impact on the country at the sight of a widow emerging from seclusion to further a cause which her husband had left only partially fulfilled. Her appeal to the voters was direct and brief: her late husband had initiated a program of reform which he could not carry through because of his untimely death; now she had come forward, in deference to the entreaties of her husband's supporters, to continue his good work. This, more than anything else, doomed the UNP's chances of electoral success. The electorate voted the SLFP to power with an absolute majority in Parliament. Mrs. Bandaranayake became the world's first woman prime minister.

The new government had promised to follow the policies of Bandaranayake, but there was, in many matters, the difficulty of determining what these policies were. The implementation of the language policy initiated by Bandaranayake occupied the first attention of the new government, which set about the task in a forthright manner. Many governmental departments were ordered to begin working in the Sinhalese language. The political problems created by this policy were still unsolved. Tamil opposition to "Sinhala-only" continued unabated and was spearheaded by the Federal Party, again confirmed by the elections as the sole spokesman of the Tamil community. The new government yielded to Tamil demands even less than Bandaranayake had done and sought to impose a solution by force. Relations between the two communities deteriorated further in this period. The Tamils resorted to extraparliamentary agitation, and the government had to take recourse to emergency powers and call out the armed forces to suppress the movement. A state of emergency declared in April, 1961, continued until May, 1963, showing an inability of the normal channels of democratic government to cope with Tamil resistance.

The new government's education policy again followed the lead given by Bandaranayake without the restraint that he would have thought politic. The unofficial Buddhist commission had recommended a state-controlled system of education throughout the country. The Buddhists had many legitimate grievances in the system as it then existed, for Christian denominations had a large number of schools maintained on funds provided by the state. In response to Buddhist demands, the government took over the management of all state-assisted denominational schools and appropriated their properties. Those schools that opted to remain outside the state system were deprived of all aid. The Christian denominations, especially the Roman Catholic Church, were most bitter at this expropriation. The Catholic congregation, by far the largest group of Christians, protested by means of civil disobedience in those areas where they were heavily concentrated. The situation was saved from deteriorating further only by an agreement between the Catholic hierarchy and the prime minister. The government, however, did not concede on the fundamentals of the reforms it had enacted. The reforms left a trail of bitterness in the Christian minority of the island.

In the sphere of economic policy, Mrs. Bandaranayake's government vigorously extended the control of the state over various aspects of the country's economy. The government moved particularly swiftly in those spheres still under the control of non-nationals. Trade in certain commodities was taken from private ownership and made a state monopoly. The balance-of-payments deficit became more acute, amounting to a near crisis. Drastic import restrictions were introduced to ease this situation. One of the beneficial results of restricting the import of certain consumer goods was the growth of local industrial ventures sheltered by the favorable tariff.

Even in the growth of local economic enterprises it was the state that played the leading role. In 1962 the government started to nationalize the insurance business. In the first stage a state monopoly of all but life insurance was declared, and then of all insurance, to become effective in January, 1964. An attempt to break into the trade in petroleum products created problems. The State Petroleum Corporation, set up by an act passed in June, 1961, appropriated for itself 25 per cent of the total business in petroleum. For this purpose the act empowered the state to nationalize the assets of the oil companies operating in Ceylon. Accordingly, some storage and distribution facilities of these companies were acquired, with compensation. The three companies operating in Ceylon—Shell, Esso, and Caltex—protested, to no avail, against this allegedly unfair competition with a state-sponsored corporation. The American and British governments protested at such treatment of the assets of their nationals. The corporation declared its intention to import oil from sources other than those hitherto used by the oil companies. Agreements were entered into with the Soviet Union, Romania, and the United Arab Republic. The effect of these changes was to alter the pattern of trade that had been in existence since British rule. The volume of trade with the countries of the West was reduced, as was also the interest of Western business interests in the island's economic prospects.

In its foreign relations the government continued with the policy of nonalignment initiated by Bandaranayake. The difficulties created by the government's economic policy resulted in closer relations with the countries of the communist bloc. When Communist China attacked India across the Himalayas, Ceylon, as the friend of both powers, attempted mediation. The prime minister took the initiative in calling a conference of neutralist nations to explore the possibilities of ending this conflict. The conference met in December, 1962, and put forward proposals for mediation, which were conveyed in person by Mrs. Bandaranayake to both capitals. Nothing came of these efforts, but they emphasized the new role of Ceylon as a state standing outside both power blocs and gave some satisfaction at the spectacle of Ceylon taking a lead in international affairs.

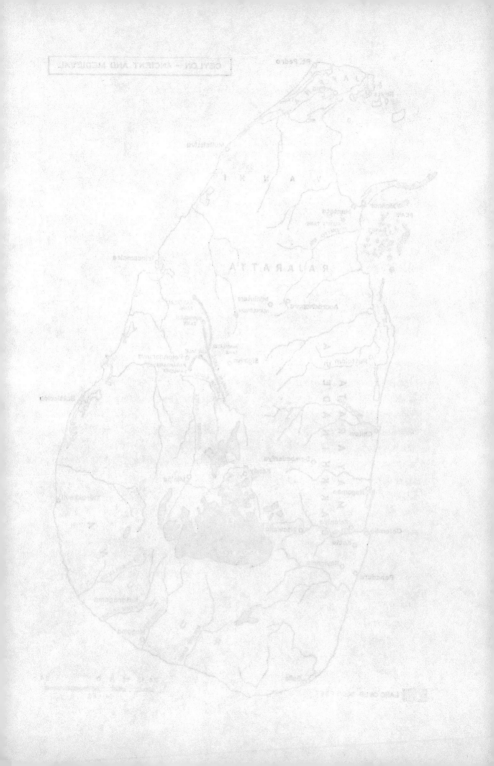

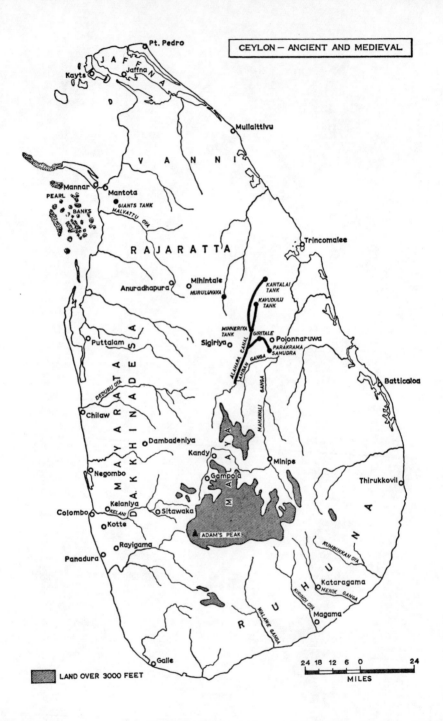

CEYLON — ANCIENT AND MEDIEVAL

Pt. Pedro
JAFFNA
Kayts
Jaffna
Mullaittivu
VANNI
Mannar
Mantota
PEARL
BANKS
GIANTS TANK
MALVATTU OYA
RAJARATTA
Trincomalee
Mihintale
KANTALAI TANK
Anuradhapura
HURULUVAVA
KAVUDULU TANK
MINNERIYA TANK
GIRITALE
Puttalam
Sigiriya
ALLAHARA CANAL
AMBAN GANGA
Polonnaruwa
PARAKRAMA SAMUDRA
MAHAWELI GANGA
Batticaloa
DEDURU OYA
Chilaw
MAYA RATA
DAKKHINA DESA
Dambadeniya
Kandy
Minipe
MALAYA
Gampola
Thirukkovil
Negombo
Kelaniya
KELANI
Sitawaka
M
Colombo
Kotte
ADAM'S PEAK
Rayigama
RUHUNA
Panadura
KUMBUKKAN OYA
Kataragama
MENIK GANGA
KIRINDI OYA
Magama
WALAWE GANGA

Galle

LAND OVER 3000 FEET

24 18 12 6 0   24
MILES

TWO

THE SINHALESE

COLONIZATION OF CEYLON
AND CONVERSION TO BUDDHISM

Sinhalese tradition, as enshrined in the chronicles of the Sinhalese, records the legendary origins of the Sinhalese race and their colonization of Ceylon. The legend relates how the daughter of a king of Vanga in northern India was carried away by a lion. The lion and the princess fell in love with each other, and out of this union were born a son and a daughter. The son, Sinhabahu, married his sister and founded a new kingdom at Sinhapura. Sinhabahu's eldest son, Vijaya, the crown prince, was of such an evil and oppressive nature that the king exiled him with seven hundred of his followers. They set out by sea and landed in Ceylon on the day of the Buddha's death. Here Vijaya established himself as ruler with the help of a native princess named Kuveni. Later he drove this woman away and summoned a princess from Madura, whom he made his queen. Maidens of high birth came from the Pandyan kingdom as wives for his followers.

The legend, with all its unlikely embellishments, enshrines the basic historical fact that in about the fifth century B.C. a band of colonists from some part of northern India, speaking an Indo-Aryan dialect, established themselves in the Ceylon littoral and were the forefathers of the Sinhalese people of Ceylon. The place names mentioned in the legend are confusing and so far apart that there has been considerable controversy on the provenance of these early colonists. Scholarly opinion, however, leans to the view that the bulk of them, and certainly those of the earliest waves, came from Gujarat in western India. Arriving by sea along the western coast, it would have been logical for them to land in the center of the west coast of Ceylon, and this is confirmed by the story in the chronicles. The frequent occurrence of place names of eastern India, together with some linguistic affinities, has given rise to the possibility of a subsequent wave of colonists from places like Bengal and Orissa. Though the legend assumes a military colonization by conquering bands, there is reason to believe that trade was also a vehicle for the colonization of Ceylon. Ceylon's wealth, especially its pearls and gems, was known in Asian trade from pre-Christian times, and it is possible that some of the merchants who came to Ceylon in search of these products decided to settle.

When these early settlers from India set foot in Ceylon, they confronted a people about whom we know very little. These people could not have been of a high standard of culture, because they have left no trace of it nor any recognizable imprint on the culture of the invaders. They probably had no strong political organization, for, unlike the Aryans in India, whose literature abounds in references to resistance and struggle with indigenous people, the Sinhalese invaders seem to have reduced the native peoples with ease and quickly established their authority. Historians are not agreed whether or not names of tribes that occur in the early literature of the Sinhalese are mythological. That there was considerable intermarriage between the Sinhalese and the aboriginal population is seen from the account of Kuveni in the Vijaya legend and from a study of Sinhalese racial types. The children born of the union between Vijaya and Kuveni are said in the legend to be the ancestors of a people called the Pulindas, who were probably a mixed race resulting from Sinhalese miscegenation. One remnant of this aboriginal population surviving in dwindling numbers today are the Veddas, a tribe of hunters living in hamlets isolated from the agricultural settlements of the Sinhalese. There must have been in the early stages a racial admixture between them and the Sinhalese. These pre-Aryan aborigines are thought to be an Australoid people, similar to the primitive inhabitants of India, whence they may well have migrated before the island was cut off from India by the sea. They were probably of the Neolithic culture, unacquainted with metal.

The evidence of the chronicles also shows that the early Sinhalese settlers were closely connected with Dravidians of the mainland. The legendary founders of the Sinhalese race, Vijaya and his followers, are said to have brought wives from the Pandyan kingdom. Thereafter it became a common practice for Sinhalese royal families to look for brides from south Indian royal dynasties. Whether Dravidian settlements in Ceylon began before or after the Sinhalese arrival is in doubt. There is, however, no doubt that the early Sinhalese settlers and indeed their descendants intermarried with Dravidians, and there was a considerable mixing of the two ethnic groups. The influence of the neighboring Dravidians on the development of Sinhalese culture and institutions was great, though not so great as to alter radically the course of this development. And because of their continuing migration to Ceylon, the Dravidians could never be absorbed into the mainstream of Sinhalese culture.

The first Sinhalese settlements were concentrated in the dry zone of the island, that area which receives a rainfall of 50 to 75 inches per year. The earliest were those to the west of Anuradhapura along the Malvattu Oya. From here they must have moved eastward down the river. Anuradhapura was very soon established as a seat of government, and the surrounding districts within a radius of about 60 to 70 miles were colonized in two centuries. Mantota was an important harbor of this period, and the Aryan colonists would have used this as an outlet to India. The early chronicles mentioned Tambapanni as the place where Vijaya landed; this has been identified as lying to the north of Puttelam. Only a little later than the Malvattu Oya settlements, if not almost contemporaneous with them, were those in the southeast, the lands watered by the Walawe Ganga, Kirindi Oya, Manik Ganga, and Kumbakkan Oya. Magama was the chief station here, and around it were several villages. Though it may have sprung up as an independent group of settlements separated from those in the north by mountain barriers, contact was soon established between the two. Another group of settlers seems to have come in through the east coast port of Trincomalee and moved down

the Mahaveli Ganga, along whose banks and tributaries they established many villages. The only settlement in the wet zone with
an independent political authority at an early stage was at Kelaniya
on the west coast along the Kelani river. By the third century b.c., all
these places were well-organized communities with established political institutions. From then on they began to establish contact with
each other and derived mutual strength and support from such contacts.

The Indo-Aryan colonists, coming from whatever part of the Indo-
Gangetic plain, would have had behind them years of experience
as settled agriculturalists. It is thus understandable that the early
settlements were riverine in character, hugging most of the important
rivers in the island. Each settlement consisted of a group of villages
where families connected to each other as a clan staked their claim
to land and set about its cultivation. Cattle breeding must have
been an important side occupation. Rice was the staple diet and the
most common grain cultivated. Water was a major problem from
the outset, as rainfall in the settlement areas was barely sufficient for
this crop. The devising of means to store water by the diversion of
rivers was already a major preoccupation of the early Sinhalese. The
fixing of village boundaries, as the colonists increased in number, is
mentioned as an important achievement of one of the earliest kings.

There must have been a need for craftsmen to provide the me-
chanical aids for agricultural activity. It might have been difficult
for the colonists to find enough craftsmen among themselves, and
here the neighboring Dravidians came to their assistance. The
Vijaya legend mentions the arrival, together with the brides from
the Pandyan kingdom, of a number of families from various guilds.
This migration of artisan and mercantile elements from south India was a constant influence on Sinhalese development.

The evolution of political institutions seems to have followed the
familiar pattern of such evolution among other Indo-Aryan tribal
groups in different parts of northern India. Kingship had not evolved
as a definite institution among the settlers at the time they settled
in Ceylon and for some time thereafter. Political authority seems
to have been vested in the *gamani*, the leader of a village or group
of villages. Among Vedic Aryans, the *gramani* was a leader of a clan

subordinate to the king. His authority was limited, and there must have been many such sources of leadership among the early settlers. But, because of the expansion of Aryan settlements into the interior and their widening geographic horizons, concentrated political authority became a necessity. In the north the ruler of Anuradhapura extended his power, brought under him other local leaders, and put forward claims to extensive recognition and the status of a kingdom. Similarly, Magama became the seat for the consolidation of authority of the southeastern settlements, and its ruler asserted himself over the chiefs of that area. Somewhat later another kingdom arose at Kelaniya. A further stage in the evolution of political authority is seen when the ruler at Anuradhapura established his overlordship over all other kingdoms. There emerged vague ideas of a suzerainty over the whole island, though not yet in actual fact. This emergence of Anuradhapura as the superior kingdom also led to the growth of what had begun as just another village into the city of Anuradhapura, the only city of the island. All these developments took place in the first three centuries of Aryan colonization. Much of it was the work of King Pandukkabhaya, whom tradition makes the successor of Vijaya.

It is reasonable to assume that the Indo-Aryan settlers would have brought with them something of the social organization prevalent in north India in the period prior to the Buddha. The Brahmanical theory of the fourfold division of society was, in practice, becoming rather blurred in the later Vedic age. The power and privileges of Brahmins continued to increase, and their influence was carried into the newly settled lands as well. They were respected members of the village community and the repositories of knowledge. As kingship grew, so also did their role as the caste which legalized kingship. Symbolic ceremonialism, much the same as it existed in India, was introduced to enhance royal authority. Education of the leaders of society was in the hands of the Brahmins. There is no evidence of the existence of the Kshatriyas as a caste among the early Sinhalese. Kshatriyas grew later as a theoretical concept to legalize the authority of the king and the ruler. Nor is there any evidence of the separation between Vaisyas and Sudras, which even in India by this time was becoming impossible to maintain.

The religious beliefs and practices of these early Sinhalese probably represented a combination of Vedic Hinduism and primitive animism, together with a smattering of the other sects familiar to them from their original homelands. The presence of the Brahmins in society must also have meant the practice of the Brahmanical religion in one form or another. The important deities of the Hindu pantheon—Brahma, Vishnu, Siva, and Indra—were worshipped in shrines erected for them. Popular religion, for which there is a great deal of evidence in the early literature, was demonistic in character. The *yaksa* cult was very prominent and became deeply entrenched into Sinhalese religious beliefs. *Yaksas* of different names were worshipped as protectors from evil. There is difference of opinion as to the nature of this belief. Some hold that *yaksas* were the pre-Aryan inhabitants of Ceylon to whom the Aryans gave supernatural attributes and worshipped for fear of being harmed by them. Others hold that it was merely a cult of ancestor worship. Of much the same category, though less common, was the Snake-god cult, worship of *nagas*. Some sects worshipped trees that were thought to possess special power. Some of the other ascetic sects found in north India seem also to have appeared in Ceylon. Jainism, the heterodoxical sect that had broken away from Brahmanism, was also known.

About three centuries after the Sinhalese colonization of Ceylon, another major influence was introduced into the island from India—the Buddhist religion. The faith that was to shape the history of the Sinhalese people was born in northeastern India in the sixth century B.C. as an intellectual reaction against the claims of the orthodox Brahmanical religion and practices. The reformation movement of Hinduism has its own complicated history and had several manifestations. The most effective of these was the religion founded by a Kshatriya prince Gotama of the Sakya clan, known among his followers as the Buddha, meaning the Enlightened One. In the main, it sought to strike a middle path between the two extremes of self-indulgence and asceticism and preached an Eightfold Path of conduct which would lead to ultimate deliverance from the chain of rebirth. The agent for the propagation of these principles was an order called the Sangha into which his disciples grouped themselves as monks. They divested themselves of all worldly ties, lived in poverty, and went about the country preaching the truths expounded by their Master. For about two centuries after its promulgation, Buddhism was just one of the sects contending for popular adherence. It gradually acquired an organization and an extensive following. The Buddhist place of worship was the *vihara*, a combination of monastery and temple, and the *stupa*, a sepulchral mound built over the relics of the Buddha and later over those of his chief disciples. The pipal tree at Gaya under which Buddha achieved enlightenment became a place of pilgrimage and worship, and the pipal itself became a sacred symbol of Buddhism.

The reign of the Emperor Asoka was a landmark in the history of Buddhism. With his conversion to Buddhism, the sect achieved the status of an official religion and enjoyed all the advantages of royal patronage and royal support. Asoka was the ruler of an empire that extended over the greater part of India, one of the largest empires in Indian history. He took it upon himself to propagate Buddhism in all parts of his extensive empire and, indeed, in the neighboring lands. Thus was launched one of the most vigorous missionary enterprises in history. One of his missions was sent to Ceylon and was headed by the *thera* (elder) Mahinda. Ceylonese tradition has it that he was a son of Asoka who had entered the Buddhist order. If this is so, Asoka must have attached great importance to this mission to convert the Sinhalese of Ceylon.

The monkish chronicles of the Sinhalese record, with miraculous accretions and dramatic effects, the mission of Mahinda and his successful conversion of Ceylon. By tradition, this event is of historic import, overshadowing even the arrival of Vijaya and his followers. Mahinda and four other *theras*, according to the Pali chronicles, came by air and landed on a hill overlooking the city of Anuradhapura. There Mahinda met King Devanampiya Tissa, who happened to pass this place on a hunting expedition. The two fell into conversation. Mahinda expounded to the king the basic tenets of the Buddhist faith and found him receptive to these new ideas. At the end of his discourse, Mahinda discovered that the king and his followers were willing to accept Buddhism. The king invited the missionary priests to his palace. Here they continued their preaching and exposition, and thousands in the royal city embraced the new faith. A few were ordained as *bhikkhus*. The king granted a royal park as residence for the ordained priesthood. This was the beginning of the Mahavihara, a historic center of Theravada Buddhism in Ceylon. In it were buildings for the use of the *bhikkhus*, and also a *stupa*—the Mahathupa, the first *stupa* to be built on the island—enshrining the collarbone of the Buddha.

Female members of the royal household showed interest in becoming nuns, and so Mahinda sent for his sister Sanghamitta to perform the ordination. She brought with her a branch of the sacred tree at Gaya under which Buddha had attained enlightenment. This branch was received with befitting ceremony and planted within the precincts of the capital city. It became thereafter an object of veneration for all Buddhists. Sanghamitta ordained the king's sister-in-law, Queen Anula, and her retinue as nuns, and a female order was also thus inaugurated. With the establishment of a male and female order of the Sangha, a *vihara* with a complex of buildings for the Sangha, and a *stupa* and sacred bo tree for the worship of the layman, the Buddhist religion was firmly implanted in Ceylon.

This dramatized version signifies more the conversion of the Sinhalese royal family than the conversion of Ceylon. It would be unhistorical to assume that Mahinda at one blow effected the conversion of the entire island. The task of taking Buddhism to the scattered rural settlements was probably begun by devoted missionaries who preceded Mahinda and certainly by many who succeeded him. Buddhism must have been known in Ceylon before the coming of Mahinda, because the Indo-Aryan settlers had been in touch with cultural developments in Aryavarta through periodic migrations and frequent commercial contacts. Contemporaneous with the conversion of Ceylon described by the chronicles, there is evidence of a southward movement of Buddhism. Inscriptions of the third century B.C. in the Deccan and south India bespeak the existence of caves of meditation for *bhikkhus*. What the chronicles pinpoint is the acceptance of Buddhism by the royal family, an event whose importance to the Sinhalese is comparable to the impact of the acceptance of this faith by Asoka on India. At a time when the power of the king was growing, together with the authority of the kingdom of Anuradhapura over the other kingdoms in the island, royal patronage of a religion would greatly hasten the spread of that religion among the people. Also important was the connection between Sinhalese Buddhism and Asoka, the first great Buddhist emperor of India. Devanampiya Tissa, even before his acceptance of Buddhism, had had connections with Asoka. He had sent an embassy to Asoka's court at Pataliputra, probably with a view to securing recognition for his assumption of consecrated royal status. This was in the tradition of Indian imperial ideas of this period, when it was the practice for rulers of unconquered petty states neighboring large empires to seek recognition of their rule from their powerful neighbor. It may also be assumed that this influence of Asoka over Tissa went a long way in the acceptance of Buddhism by the Sinhalese king.

The significance of the manner of royal conversion was that, following the Asokan pattern, a close link was forged between the state and Buddhism. Buddhism, indeed, became the established religion of the Sinhalese kingdom. Tissa, it is said, desired the religion to be established in such a way that he and his subjects could live within the order of the Buddha. Such establishment of Buddhism in a country was evidently a new departure in the history of that religion and seems to have been an innovation of Asoka. It meant in effect the existence of institutions of Buddhism, supported from the coffers of the state, close to the royal palace, exerting a deep influence on royal policy. It became incumbent on succeeding kings to protect and provide for the growing institutions of the Buddhist church. It called into existence an influential group in the capital, the Sangha, which could influence royal policy and to whom in turn the kings became morally accountable for their actions.

The chronicles also relate that Mahinda insisted that the religion would be fully established in Ceylon only when someone of Ceylonese descent studied the *Vinaya* (Buddhist scripture) and expounded it. This was no doubt a later interpolation by chroniclers of the fifth century A.D. Yet it is enlightening for what it tells us of the growth of a nationalistic form of Buddhism in the centuries after its establishment. It demonstrates an early attempt to "Ceylonize" the Buddhist church and reduce its dependence on the land of its origin, and to show that the Sangha must consist primarily of sons of the soil in order to become permanently established. Consequently, the account goes on, Arittha, the nephew of the king, a Ceylonese well versed in the *Vinaya*, ceremonially expounded the doctrine at an assembly of *bhikkhus*, and Mahinda's last condition was fulfilled.

In a more concrete sense, the coming of Buddhism to Ceylon helped the growth of a Sinhalese cultural individuality. The missionary character of the new religion, its attempts to appeal to man's mind and gain his adherence led it to adopt certain methods which left an imprint on the people. The preaching of sermons and the ideas conveyed in them were an effective means of mass education. This was a major feature of Asokan missionary methods in all parts of India and indeed marks the first attempts at popular education, in contrast to the abstract speculations and exclusive theology of Brahmanism. What Buddhism did to India, it may be said to have done more intensively in Ceylon. The most notable contribution is seen in the development of language. In India, Buddhism made its appeal through the vernacular of each people it addressed, as opposed to Sanskrit, which was the sole and not universally understood medium of Brahmanism. The language of the early Sinhalese, an Indo-Aryan dialect, was intelligible to the missionaries from India, who thus found it easy to address themselves to the people. From the early beginnings, the task of writing the scriptures in Sinhalese was attempted. This marks the beginning of a literary Sinhalese language. The Asokan script was also introduced at this time. Pali was the language of the Buddhist scriptures and was therefore studied by the Sinhalese literati. It influenced deeply the growth of the Sinhalese language.

The introduction of Buddhism also started the construction of large, permanent buildings for its various institutions. The first constructions, the *sangharama* (monastery) and the *stupa* in the spot granted to Mahinda, marked the beginning of ever-increasing activity in religious building. Kings looked upon it as a duty to build for the glory of the faith. It became part of the concept of state religion. Very soon the designs of Buddhist buildings brought from India were being transformed by Sinhalese individuality. Buddhist monuments now took a new line of development in Ceylon, and the results of this are a valuable contribution to the cultural heritage of mankind.

Less tangible, though no less important, was the undoubted influence that the acceptance of the new faith had on the standards of conduct in society. A people who were largely animistic in their beliefs, fearing and seeking to propitiate natural phenomena that surrounded them, would not have developed any high moral values in their daily life. Divested of its theology, Buddhism provided a code of ethics of great value for civilized life. No doubt the new religion often had to come to terms with powerfully rooted indigenous cults. But it raised these crude beliefs and built them into the Buddhist system. The presence of the members of the Sangha in even the smallest villages was a moralizing influence on the life of the village community. This is in sharp contrast to the traditional influence of the Brahmin, who was not of the people in the way that a *bhikkhu* was, and, in any case, there were not many Brahmins in ancient Ceylon.

The Indo-Aryan tribes, by migrating to an island from their mainland home, developed individualistic traits that, over the ages, distinguished them increasingly from their ancestral kin. They developed a separate language and separate institutions and were subject to influences unlike those which touched the other Indo-Aryan tribes of north India. Now the spread of Buddhism among the people gave another major boost to their individuality. Though it is true that Buddhism came as part of a movement that swept over all India, its character in Ceylon was different in its nature and intensity. Thus, while in India the next wave of Brahmanism and the assimilating quality of Hinduism removed Buddhism as an institutional religion, in Ceylon Buddhism grew untroubled by such influences, acquired a new shape given to it by the Sinhalese people, and in turn gave the Sinhalese a new face. The succeeding centuries are thus the history of Sinhalese Buddhism in Ceylon.

THE CLASSICAL AGE, 200 B.C.–A.D. 1200

Growth of Political Power and Institutions

The years following the introduction and spread of Buddhism in Ceylon witnessed the growth of Sinhalese political power. The kingdom at Anuradhapura, helped in part by the influx of new ideas and new policies, increased in strength and its kings in political stature.

In about the second century B.C., the threat of external danger gave
further cohesion to the Sinhalese kingdom. Dravidian influence had
been felt in considerable extent in Ceylon from the earliest Aryan
colonization. After Tissa, the first Buddhist king, some Dravidian
Tamil adventurers seized the throne at Anuradhapura, thus in-
terrupting the succession of Sinhalese rulers who traced their descent to the legendary Vijaya. The defeat of one of these Tamil rulers, Elara, and the restoration of Sinhalese sovereignty has been regarded as an epic event in Sinhalese historical tradition. The victor,
Duttugemunu, is treated as a hero in national lore, and his name is
remembered up to modern times. His defeat of Elara in the final personal combat dramatizes this recapture of power at Anuradhapura.
In actual fact, however, this was only one episode in a recurrent
phenomenon of Sinhalese-Tamil rivalry in the island. The Tamil
challenge so decisively defeated here was only temporarily disposed
of. In later years we see, off and on, Tamil invaders from the neighboring mainland wresting power for short periods. But the myth of
the Duttugemunu-Elara combat was nurtured in monkish tradition to feed a religio-communal nationalism of the still scattered
Sinhalese people. The story emphasizes that Duttugemunu was
a champion of Buddhism and fought to re-establish this faith and
extirpate Hindu heresy supported by the Tamil rulers. It goes on
to attribute to this king a number of Buddhist monuments, at
least some of which are known on other evidence to have been built
after his time. The moral of the story is clear. It marks the beginnings of Sinhalese nationalism and of the idea that the island must
be preserved as a seat of Sinhalese political power and monopolized
by the Buddhist faith.

This nationalism was translated into political terms as an aspira-
tion for an all-island sovereignty. The former loose relationship between three semi-independent kingdoms in the north, southwest,
and southeast gave place to a more rigorous assertion of the control
of Anuradhapura over the rest of the country. The city now became
the capital of the island in a real sense. No doubt, the extent of its
control over the other regions depended on the personality of the
ruler and the strength of his own kingdom. But gradually an administrative machinery was evolved embracing the whole country. The

country around Anuradhapura was the king's country, Rajaratta, and it is here that we see the most important developments in politics and culture. Anuradhapura remained the capital until the eleventh century, when the capital was shifted to Polonnaruwa a few miles to the east. In many respects this was the classical age of Sinhalese power, when, in spite of the many political vicissitudes, great achievements were recorded in the various fields of culture. Even after the capital shifted to Polonnaruwa, it was this northern, dry zone of the island that remained the important home of Sinhalese civilization.

One of the results of this political consolidation was the enhancement in the role and position of royalty. The kings of the Sinhalese kingdoms during these centuries arose from a few noble clans. The most ancient of these clans was that which traced descent from the legendary founders of the first Sinhalese kingdom and ruled, with interruptions, until the tenth century. Another family of rulers was the Moriya line, which was probably connected with the more famous dynasty of that name in India. Then there was the Lambakanna dynasty, probably a branch of the old royal clan. All these dynasties traced their descent, in keeping with the Indian practice, from the sun or the moon. The Brahmanical concept of sovereignty, the right of the Kshatriyas to rule, was firmly planted and accepted in theory by Buddhism.

Most of the external symbolism of royalty was practiced in the Indian manner as it was laid down in the Brahmanical texts. The diadem, umbrella, and throne were all used. The *abisheka*, or ceremony of consecration, was faithfully performed. So were other ceremonies marking auspicious occasions in court. All this gave a certain importance to the Brahmin in the Buddhist kingdom. There were a few Brahmins in the capital to perform these functions and even to advise the kings. We hear of the *purohita*, an important person in the Hindu state, though certainly not as influential in a Buddhist state. It seems likely that the education of princes was partly in the hands of Brahmin priests, who, because of their Sanskrit learning, were good instructors in the science of statecraft. The *Arthasastra*, the classic Hindu text on polity, was well known to Sinhalese kings. Yet the influence of the Brahmins on royalty was more

formal than substantial and does not in any way compare with the
influence exerted by the Buddhist priesthood. Brahmins performed
the various royal sacrifices, but their functions did not extend very
much further.

We can discern a movement toward the sanctity of the person of
the monarch, a result of the influence of the Sanskritic tradition of
kingship. This is first noticeable in the gradual adoption of the more
and more extravagant titles that were being evolved in India. Thus
the plain *rajah* becomes *maharajah* (great king), *rajadhirajan* (ruler
of kings), and even *Mahipati* (Lord of the Earth). Soon after the acceptance in India of the idea of the divinity of the king's person, the
concept gained currency in Ceylon. The later kings of Anuradhapura
were styled *deva*, or god. The emphasis on tracing descent from
the solar or lunar dynasty is also an index to this trend. In a later
period, after the twelfth century, the divinity of the monarch was
further emphasized in inscriptions and literary works. The title then
used by the kings was *cakravartin*, or universal emperor. A fusion of
these essentially Brahmanical ideas of kingship with Buddhism is
witnessed in the claim sometimes put forward to descent from Ma-
hasammata, the Buddhist originator of kingship. Later kings also put
forward the claim that they were Boddhisattvas, beings who were des-
tined to become Buddhas according to later Buddhist theology.

The law of succession is not clear. While there are many instances
of hereditary succession, there are also several cases of succession
from brother to brother. The latter was a deviation from the Indian practice, where primogeniture was the recognized means of succession. This absence of a generally accepted law seems to have been
the cause of many disputed successions in medieval Ceylon. There
are many instances of wars between scions of the royal family for
the throne. Thus, the medieval Sinhalese kingdoms had a somewhat
bloody and checkered history. Because of the establishment of Buddhism as the official religion, one basic qualification for kingship was
that the incumbent had to be a practicing Buddhist. It was important that a candidate to the throne have the support of the clergy.
Particularly in cases of disputed succession, the influence of the
clergy could tilt the scales one way or another. It is also obvious that
the aspirant to kingship must have the support of the nobility,

for the rulers had to rely heavily on the nobles for various functions of government.

The Sinhalese monarchy was despotic in character, and the king was in both theory and practice the source of all authority. His powers were comparable with those of the rulers of contemporary Hindu kingdoms of India, with this difference: that, owing to the compactness of the country and the homogeneity of their subjects, the Sinhalese kings were able to exert more personal authority. Checks to the arbitrary exercise of royal absolutism were much the same in Ceylon as they were in India. However sacrosanct the person of the monarch, it did not rule out the probability of rebellion against an unpopular tyrant. Examples of such uprisings in Ceylonese history are abundant. Just as the Hindu monarch was bound by the Hindu Dharma (law), so the Sinhalese king had to rule according to the Buddhist Dharma. The influence wielded by the Brahmins in a Hindu state is comparable with that wielded by the Buddhist priests in the Sinhalese kingdom. They were the guardians of the Buddha *sasana* (Order), and they would see to it that kings did not flout the Dharma in their state policies.

A council of state consisting of the major administrative officers of the kingdom was in attendance in a purely advisory capacity. There was a fair amount of departmentalization of administrative duties. Ministers or officers in charge of each of these dealt personally with the king and received their instructions from him. The number of departments whose names occur in inscriptional and literary sources of the time is very great. Their wide range shows that the state undertook numerous functions and had effective means of controlling and directing the life of the community. Ministers were in all probability members of noble families, but there is no evidence that they had hereditary claim to office. Kings were nearly always firmly in control of the appointment and dismissal of ministers during the period when the Sinhalese kingdom was at the height of its power. Members of the royal family held the highest positions in administration. The *yuvaraja* was the heir to the throne and was given responsible office. He was sometimes posted as the viceroy of a province.

The army was an important instrument of royal policy and the major prop of absolutism. Its commander-in-chief, or *senapati*, was thus nearest to the king, and the office was generally held by one of his close relatives. The great mass of military titles that occur in contemporary sources also attests to the deep knowledge of military strategy and the arts of warfare. Indian texts on the subject were widely known. A large standing army was a necessity, considering the frequent threats to the king's position from external and internal sources. The army consisted of both mercenaries and militia. Mercenaries were paid soldiers of various races and tribes recruited from both Ceylon and south India. Besides Sinhalese there were Tamils, Keralas, and Kannadigas. The regular militia was recruited from the rural population on a cantonment basis. Each canton had to provide and equip a certain number of men. Needless to say, their training and equipment were not comparable to that of the mercenaries, who therefore bore the brunt of any real fighting. Levies of militiamen were used more for preserving public peace and safeguarding royal property, and they often undertook civilian functions as well.

Whenever the country was united under one scepter, provincial administration was well organized. For a greater part of the period the country was divided into three parts: Rajaratta, Dakkhinadesa, and Ruhuna. The central highlands, or Malaya, formed a separate region in which the control of the monarch at Anuradhapura was little felt. It was in any case not properly occupied until the later medieval period. Prior to this it was mainly the home of rebels and fugitives from the settled parts. The major regions were further subdivided into cantons (*mandala*) and districts (*rattha*). Headmen were appointed over each of these units and were the chief administrative officers. The organization of regional government is comparable to that of the Pallava kingdom of south India, with which the Sinhalese had considerable contact. The Pallava system in turn derives from that evolved under the Gupta empire which preceded it in northern India. At the lowest level of local government was the village community. It managed its own affairs with little interference from the central administration. At the village level there was a good deal of popular participation in government, though the more influential offices were probably monopolized by a few of the wealthier landowning families. The independence of the village in the administrative organization enabled it to pursue its own life relatively unaffected by the vicissitudes to which the central government was subject.

One of the signs of strength of the Sinhalese kingdom was the growth of its external contacts. After the decline of Buddhism in northern India, contacts with that region were less intense. Relations are in evidence with the Kalingas and with Andhra where, under the Satavahanas, Buddhism flourished in the first centuries of the Christian era. Also because of the Buddhist ties, diplomatic relations were established with the Burmese kingdom of Ramanna, and in the twelfth century an expedition was launched against this kingdom by Parakrama Bahu I over some difference that had arisen between them. It was with the Dravidian kingdoms of south India, however, that relations were continuous and close, both in friendship and hostility. Kings frequently procured brides and recruited soldiers from these regions. The first traditional record of a Sinhalese king's interference in south Indian affairs occurs in the reign of Gaja Bahu in the second century A.D., when legends attribute to him a successful expedition against the Chola kingdom. Tamil literature refers to his presence in the court of the Chera king, Senguttuvan, at a ceremonial occasion. In the fifth century A.D. there occurred a Pandyan invasion of the island, as a result of which the Sinhalese kingdom of Anuradhapura fell into the hands of the Pandyan warriors, who ruled in succession for about 25 years. The liberation of the kingdom was the achievement of Dhatusena.

In the seventh century A.D. the Sinhalese became deeply involved in the politics of southern India, entering into political alliances with the kingdoms of that region. Disputants to the throne went across the straits and returned with troops to fight out their claims. Kings such as Dathopatissa I (643-50), Dathopatissa II (659-67), and Aggabodhi III (633-43) owed their thrones to the support of Tamil mercenaries. One of the closest alliances was forged when Manavamma, a claimant to the Sinhalese throne, betook himself to the Pallava court to win the friendship of the reigning monarch, Narasimhavarman I. In response to Manavamma's request, the Pallava king fitted out an expedition to Ceylon to help him win the throne. The expedition succeeded in driving out the ruler of Anu-radhapura and installing Manavamma on the throne. But before Manavamma could consolidate his position, the Pallava army had to return because their own king was critically ill. Manavamma there-upon retreated to south India once more and returned 20 years later with a force provided by the next Pallava king, Narasimhavarman II. This attempt was a success, and Manavamma was consecrated king in A.D. 684. These events initiated a period of Pallava-Sinhalese politi-cal alliance, with fruitful consequences in nonpolitical matters as well.

In the ninth century there was active contact between the Sinhalese and the Pandyan kingdom, which was then supreme in the far south of India. The Pandyan king, Srivallabba, invaded Ceylon in the mid-dle of the century, sacked the capital, and returned, having con-cluded a treaty with the reigning king, Sena I (833-53). In the reign of his successor, Sena II (853-87), we find a reversal of roles, and the Sinhalese appeared in south India as sponsors of a candidate to the Pandyan throne. The son of the Pandyan monarch who had invaded Ceylon, Varaguna, appeared to ask for aid against his father. The Sinhalese king, seeing an opportunity to avenge the earlier invasion, consented and fitted out an expeditionary force. This force landed in south India at the time that the Pandyan king was heavily engaged against a Pallava invasion of his dominion. It seized and sacked Madura, the Pandyan capital, and set up Varaguna as king. The Sinhalese were able to recover much of the treasure seized during the earlier invasion. This Pandya-Sinhalese alliance took Sinhalese sol-diers once more to the mainland in A.D. 915. The Pandyan king, Rajasimha II, was being pressed by the Cholas, who were on the rise in south India. He appealed for assistance to the Sinhalese king, Kassapa V (914-23). Kassapa sent a force in response, but this time the combined Pandyan-Sinhalese army was defeated by the Cholas at the battle of Vellur. The Sinhalese lost their commander in battle and withdrew their troops to Ceylon. In the reign of Kassapa's suc-cessor, Dappula IV (924-35), the King Rajasimha II was overthrown by the Cholas and sought refuge in the Sinhalese court. Dappula was eager to give him an army to regain his kingdom, but the nobles opposed it. So Rajasimha quit the country, leaving behind the Pandyan diadem and regalia.

Now the Sinhalese kingdom attracted the attention of the powerful Chola empire. Its alliance with the Pandyans made the Cholas view it with hostility. The Chola king demanded the Pandyan royal insignia from the Sinhalese, who rejected the demand. Thereupon the Chola king, Parantaka, invaded Ceylon, drove the king from Anuradhapura, and sacked the city. Invasions of Ceylon now became more frequent and were caused by the growing strength of the kingdoms of south India and their attraction for the wealth of the island. In 958 the Rastrakuta king, Krishna III, invaded north Ceylon and took back considerable booty. In the following year there was an unsuccessful attempt at invasion by the Chola monarch. The Sinhalese political decline that set in soon afterward was an open invitation to the Cholas, who had by then built up a powerful navy and dominated the south Indian seas. Rajaraja I invaded the island in 993 with full force, captured the king, and annexed the royal province of Rajaratta to the Chola empire. Later on he expanded southward and annexed Ruhuna as well. Organized resistance by the descendants of the royal line soon began. In 1070 the Sinhalese reasserted their independence under Vijayabahu.

The Cholas had shifted the capital to Polonnaruwa, which was better situated to control the southern part of the country where resistance was being organized. Later Sinhalese kings retained this city as their capital. Under the able ruler Vijayabahu (1070-1110), the Sinhalese kingdom soon recovered from the ravages caused by the Chola invasion. It soon reached new heights under one of the greatest monarchs of early Sinhalese history. Parakrama Bahu I (1153-86) was perhaps the ablest ruler of this period. His reputation in Sinhalese tradition is second only to that of Duttugemunu, but his fame rests on more solid achievements. He conducted an active foreign policy. He carried out an invasion of the Burmese kingdom of Ramanna in 1164-65, with whose king the Sinhalese had outstanding disputes. He interfered in the politics of south India, sponsoring the cause of a claimant to the Pandyan throne. His armies waged an extensive campaign on south Indian soil, at first with great success, though la-

ter he met with reverses and his protégé was defeated. Under him
Sinhalese naval power was undoubtedly the strongest in its history,
as shown by his ability to undertake these expeditions abroad.

Thus, it is clear that the Sinhalese kingdom was in almost continuous contact with the powers of southern India. In its classical
period, Ceylon was able to withstand the attempted penetration of
powers from the mainland. Though it went under for brief periods,
it soon reasserted itself with renewed rigor and by its exertions succeeded, except for the 75 years of Chola conquest, in maintaining its
independence for centuries. The fact that the threat came mainly
from the Tamil kingdoms across the straits served to keep alive the
vision of the Tamils as the enemy of the Sinhalese people. This myth
had been cultivated under Duttugemunu and was writ into Sinhalese
political tradition. Thus it was that a people who had very close cultural relations with each other were cast politically in the role of
antagonists. By retaining their independence, the Sinhalese were
enabled to develop their distinctive strand of civilization, though
they owed much to Dravidian influences.

Development of Social and Economic Organization

The social organization that the immigrant Sinhalese brought with
them was changed under the influences of independent political
power and isolation from India. We saw above that the Brahmanical
concept of caste was not valid even at the earliest stages of Sinhalese
history. It became even less valid as Sinhalese society developed. In
theory, it was sought now and again to squeeze the Sinhalese caste
system into the Brahmanical structure, at least with respect to the
higher castes. In particular, with the growth of royal power, we see
the emergence of Kshatriya claims. Only a Kshatriya could become
king, and he became eligible only if he had a Kshatriya maiden by his
side. The claim seems to have originated among the noble families
of some of the clans that migrated to Ceylon. Only members of these
clans could aspire to kingship. Originally, they must have been the
warriors in the tribe, though later, with the growth of a standing army, they were divested of this function. They would also have
been prominent landlords and holders of high administrative posts.
None of the other three Brahmanical castes was relevant to Sinhalese

social structure, and even these Kshatriyas in the later periods merged into the social structure that evolved in the course of years.

As it developed, the division of Sinhalese society into caste groups was not as deep as in India and was far more humanitarian. This is due to both political and religious causes. The maintenance of independence and unity of the country for long periods, with but brief interruptions, did not foster the growth of a divided society. The persistent presence of royal absolutism in both theory and practice did not permit the growth of groups with privileges or status too far above the mass of the people. Even when divisions did arise, they were not allowed to become harsh and oppressive as in India because of Buddhism. Buddhism admitted of no built-in, natural divisions in humanity. Consequently, social taboos against the lower orders of society were kept within bounds and, in any case, were not given a religious sanction as in India. But we should not overestimate the influence of Buddhism as a leveler of social distinctions. In this respect, Hindu influences in society were quite strong, and the Sinhalese may be said to have shared the contemporary Indian attitude to the relationship between the individual and groups in society. Yet these two factors—political and religious—resulted in the development of caste among the Sinhalese as a system distinct from that of most Indian societies. If any comparison is to be made with India, it could be more fruitfully applied to the south Indian system, where the Brahmanical theory was also largely irrelevant.

Among the Sinhalese, the major division in society was between agricultural and nonagricultural occupations. Those engaged in agriculture were the highest groups in society. The *govi*, or cultivator, belonged to the highest caste and remains so today. Among these were divisions of status, the topmost being the chiefs who held administrative office, next the titled men, and finally the peasant farmer. As there were no further subdivisions, this caste thus formed a compact body, comprising a great majority of the Sinhalese people. This resulted in a great simplicity in the caste structure, as contrasted with the complexities of the Indian system. The tradition grew that cultivation of the soil was the most noble occupation, and he who owned and tilled a plot of land was of noble birth. He could not aspire to the throne, but he was near the seat of power. Being the most populous and the most influential group, their support was essential to royal absolutism.

The nonagricultural people were considered of lower rank—*hina*. They were divided into a number of groups, varying at different periods, on an occupational basis. As new functions appeared in society, new castes arose. Occupations were hereditary, and these castes were endogamous. Each caste lived in its own village or section of the village. In towns, they lived along particular streets, as in south India. The status of each caste was determined according to the nature of the function it performed and shifted over time according to the economic importance of this function. One possible origin of some castes could have been from immigrant groups who either came with a special function or acquired one in the island. Many of the professional castes were self-regulating to a great degree.

The lowest caste was the *chandalas*, who performed the meanest occupation like sweeping streets, removing refuse, and carrying corpses. They were segregated in separate villages. They were the only caste that corresponded to the untouchable castes of India, though the idea of pollution by touch was not taken to such extremes. The institution of slavery was prevalent among the Sinhalese. Its origin is obscure. A good number of the slaves must have been captured in war. Some had sold themselves into slavery to pay off debts. Members of the nobility and other wealthy people had a number of slaves in their possession. Slaves were sometimes assigned to monasteries and temples. Yet slaves could redeem themselves and become free men once more. There is every evidence of the humane treatment meted out to slaves.

With the cultivators occupying the highest status and being most numerous, the Sinhalese were a great agrarian society with a long and interesting history of agricultural activity. The early Sinhalese settlers brought with them their knowledge of rice cultivation and soon settled down to this occupation in their new homes. The earliest farmers made use of the rains that fell in the north toward the end of the year to cultivate an annual crop. This practice was continued and remains a popular method of cultivation in many parts of the island today. Clearing of jungle and opening of virgin land for farming was a major activity in early times. The progress from dry to wet cultivation was a major step and must have been caused by intensive colonization and denser population of fertile tracts. The undependable character of the seasonal northeast monsoon and the prolonged periods of drought caused problems of water shortage and were a spur to Sinhalese ingenuity in the conservation of water. Thus we find the Sinhalese embarking on ventures to conserve water and augment the available supply of water from earliest times.

The development of this aspect of technology was influenced by many sources. The Aryan settlers themselves would have brought some of it from India. Early Sanskrit literature gives evidence of a knowledge of irrigation as practiced in the Ganges valley. Dravidian knowledge must also have been available to the Sinhalese. Southern India was quite well irrigated from the beginnings of the Christian era, and Dravidian artisans were readily available. There is also reason to believe that there was some indigenous knowledge from pre-Aryan times, because the early legends talk of tanks (reservoirs). Using these sources as a beginning, the native genius of the Sinhalese people worked to develop and fashion almost to perfection the technique of water storage. Over a period of a millennium and a half were constructed irrigation works of varying sizes from the colossal to the smallest. Some of these remain to the present day and function for the same purposes as they did many centuries ago. Even those that have been damaged by time are of such quality that they can be repaired and put back into operation. These irrigation works constitute one of the greatest legacies of ancient Sinhalese civilization.

Two different irrigation systems are distinguishable. The first was the relatively straightforward method of constructing a dam across a stream or a river and storing the water below it. From here the water was carried in a main channel from which innumerable channels would branch out, taking the water to fields below the reservoir. By the second method, part of the water of a flowing river was diverted through long channels, conveying it to a reservoir at a more suitable or useful place for storage and irrigation. In both systems there was a wide range of possibilities from the small village work tapping a seasonal stream to the huge reservoir storing water from the large perennial rivers.

The earliest works were largely of the first type, which intercepted the waters of a village stream by an earthen embankment. With the advance in technical knowledge, larger permanent stone dams were built. A small tank very soon became—and remains—the feature of almost every village in the northern area. These were probably the result of private effort undertaken communally by the landowners of the village. Later on there is evidence of private individuals undertaking the construction of these tanks, owning them, and deriving the benefits from the issue of water to farmers in the fields below. Insufficient rains would have caused many of them to dry up, and very few of these small works would have made possible two crops a year in the fields they watered.

With the increase in royal power and the formation of strong states, more ambitious works of irrigation were begun with royal initiative. From the first century A.D. onwards, there ruled a number of tank-building kings who are remembered in Sinhalese lore for their irrigation works. The earliest large tanks were built by King Vasabha (67-111 A.D.), and their perimeter was two to three miles. The first canal is also mentioned at this time—the Alahara canal, which took water from the Amban Ganga for a distance of 30 miles. Another achievement of the same period was the construction of underground channels to carry water to the bathing tanks in the capital city. These enterprises bespeak the first significant advances in hydraulic construction. They reveal a knowledge of the technique of calculating gradients and of contouring and leveling. The building of permanent stone dams across rivers had also been mastered by then.

Further remarkable progress was achieved in the reign of King Mahasena (275-301). Among tanks and canals traditionally attributed to him are some of the most spectacular products of the whole Sinhalese civilization. The first of these is the Minneriya tank, which utilized as feeder the Alahara canal excavated two centuries earlier and extended and enlarged it. The large tank thus fed by this canal had an area of 4,670 acres. A major source of water throughout Sinhalese history, it remained unbreached until modern times. Early in the twentieth century it was restored and used to irrigate the lands around it and is now the nucleus of a flourishing agricultural colony. Almost as large, though not equally permanent, was the

Kavadulu tank, which stored waters of the river of the same name. Another large tank built by this king, the Huruluwewa, has also been repaired and is now used for irrigation. The people living in the vicinity of the Minneriya tank deified this monarch and worshipped him in a temple erected near the tank.

From Mahasena onward, Sinhalese kings looked upon the construction and maintenance of irrigation works as an intrinsic part of their duty toward their subjects. They extended tanks and canals already in existence. Another assiduous tank-builder was Dhatusena (459-77). The largest tank he built was the Kalavava, with an area of over 6,000 acres. A canal 54 miles in length took water from this tank to Tissawewa in Anuradhapura, irrigating the lands between. Another massive undertaking of the same period was the tank now known as Giant's Tank, which tapped the waters of the Aruvi Aru and diverted them into the reservoir by means of a canal 17 miles long. This tank was one of the earliest and largest to be built in the flat country to the north of the dry zone. With later extensions it irrigated over 14,000 acres of land and has been almost continuously used until the present day.

In the sixth century considerable tank-building activity was spearheaded by two kings, Mogallana II (531-51) and Aggabodhi I (574-604). A large tank was built about seven miles southeast of Anuradhapura by damming the Malvattu Oya. Steps were also taken to augment the capacity of the Nuvaravava, which provided water to the citizens of the capital city. Another large tank in the Mullaitivu district, northeast of Anuradhapura, was built at this time, tapping the waters of the Manal Aru. There was a wide extension of the network of feeding canals to enlarge existing tanks and create new sources of supply. One new tank thus built was the Kantalay tank, which was fed by a canal 29 miles long leading out of the Minneriya tank constructed three centuries earlier. Similarly another tank, the Giritale tank, was constructed from a branch of the Alahara canal feeding the old Minneriya tank. This brought into being an irrigation network with the Amban Ganga as its main source, supplemented by the tributaries of the Amban Ganga and by other rivers, filling first one large tank and then another, thus eliminating all waste and making use of every surplus. Four large tanks were created by this system, and there was a total of 95 miles of canals.

By the end of the seventh century, many of the great sources of water supply in the dry zone had been tapped. Kings in subsequent years devoted their efforts to keeping these works in good repair and extending them wherever possible. The supply sources of existing tanks were increased by tapping other streams that lay in the vicinity. A number of extension works were carried out in the ninth century by Sena II (853-87), the most notable among them being the work done at Minipe. There was a lull in irrigation development during the tenth and eleventh centuries, largely attributable to the foreign invasions and unrest that characterized these years. There is also reason to believe that the temporary breakdown of central authority resulted in the decline of this vast irrigation system. Apart from the damage caused by the lack of proper maintenance and care, there was also wanton destruction of tank bunds by rival forces.

The next period of activity coincided with the re-emergence of centralized power at Polonnaruwa. Vijaya Bahu I, who initiated this revival, repaired many breached tanks. He restored the Minneriya-Kantalay system and a number of other lesser tanks. In a galaxy of great tank-builders the name of Parakrama Bahu I shines with a record of achievement unparalleled by others. In the early part of his reign he concentrated his energies in the region known as Dakkhinadesa, which lies in the southwest of the dry zone. Here he dammed the principal river, Deduru Oya, at three places and built storage tanks. After he became king of the whole island, he extended his tank construction to the heart of the dry zone. The most outstanding work of the reign was the Parakramasamudra (sea of Parakrama) at Polonnaruwa, formed by damming the Amban Ganga at another point and leading the waters from there by canal. It also received excess water from the older Giritale tank. This tank had an area of over 5,000 acres and irrigated 18,000 acres. It is one of the major restored works of modern Ceylon. He built a number of other tanks and repaired and restored almost all the earlier works, which were in a dilapidated state. At the end of his reign the whole irrigation system of the dry zone was working to full capacity.

As a large part of our sources for a knowledge of Sinhalese history are of monkish origin, there is no evidence available on the technique of constructing irrigation works. There must have been some theoretical knowledge, some manuals on this science, on which practical building could be based. The selection of rivers and points at which to dam them, the calculation of gradients for the sloping of channels, must have demanded technical knowledge and the use of instruments of a nature comparable to modern hydraulics. The massive dams were broad-based and built in such a way as to withstand heavy water pressure. The art of consolidating and strengthening dams was mastered.

The construction of water outlets and their control was another major achievement of early Sinhalese engineering. The main feature was a well dug at a spot near the crest of the dam (*bisokotuva*). It had two culverts, one through which water passed into the well and one discharging the water to the outer slope. The flooring and walls of the well were of slabs of stone that fitted exactly. To control the water that flowed out of the well there was a lock or valve of the sluice made of wood. It was the early discovery of this system of wells and sluices that enabled the Sinhalese builders to construct larger and larger works, for the problem of control of the outflow of water had thus been mastered.

Another remarkable feature of these constructions is the leading of water for long distances through canals and channels. By the twelfth century there were about 600 miles of canals leading out of the major rivers, besides those connected to smaller works. The trapezoidal channels were most effectively designed for the flow of water. The interconnection of various natural waterways by these canals called for tremendous technical skill in calculating gradients and in contour leveling. There were also the problems of assembling and transporting labor and building materials. Most of the material was cut or hewn stone; the elephant must have done much of the transporting, as, indeed, it still does in the rural areas. We do not know how so much labor was made available at the sites of large works.

The maintenance of the large works and the distribution of the available water probably necessitated a large bureaucracy. An officer called "Inspector of Reservoir," mentioned in the inscriptions, was responsible for such work. We also hear of officials in charge of apportioning water from the main channels to individual plots and collecting dues from the owners. So that the water might be used economically and brought to the proper fields at the appropriate time, there had to be a good deal of advance planning in cultivation. A number of officers at the village level attended to this. Certain regulations governing the cultivation of irrigated plots in a district were formulated by the officers and had to be strictly followed. Thus, fields fed by a particular channel had to be plowed and made ready for cultivation at the same time, so that all could make use of the water when it was diverted into the channel. There were strict penalties against unauthorized tapping of water from the channels.

The irrigation works of the ancient Sinhalese provide some of the few links between the old and the new Ceylon. Many of the works noted above are in use today. This legacy of their early civilization has appealed to the imagination of the modern Sinhalese, who feel a sense of pride in such achievements. It has also served the cause of the backward-looking nationalists among them who, on the basis of this evidence, point to a period of glory and prosperity destroyed only by the advent of foreign elements. There is a natural tendency to exaggerate the scope of the old irrigation system, to assume that all the works were in full operation at one and the same time. On the basis of this assumption, wild guesses have been made regarding the size of the population that the system supported. Even more dangerous is the assumption that, if only all these works could be restored and the farmer diverted to the dry zone from the overpopulated sea coasts, Ceylon's economic problems would be solved. The repopulation of Ceylon's dry zone is seen today not merely as an economic venture but also as an attempt to recapture the past.

Proprietary and tenurial rights in land in the classical period were very similar to those of India. Traditional Hindu theory pronounced that the king, as "Lord of the Earth," was entitled to a share of the produce from the tiller of the soil in return for royal protection. This share was generally reckoned as a sixth part of the harvest. Together with the ideas of kingship came Indian theories of royal rights over land. As in India, the king's rights over land, no doubt, grew gradually. In the beginning, when the land was just being opened up and no facilities for irrigation were provided, the rights of the sovereign could not be and did not have to be asserted forcefully. But when the irrigation system reached its peak and agriculture in the dry zone was being carried on to its maximum capacity, we find hereditary ownership and cultivation of land. A few wealthy men owned large tracts of land in diverse forms of tenure, and the majority of tenants lived on the land and cultivated it on the basis of different kinds of tenure.

Those who could be termed landlords had come to own their land in different ways. The most valued form of tenure, known as *pamunu*, was one in which the owner had hereditary rights over the land. These lands could be transferred and were subject only to a nominal tax of recognition to the king. In the older villages the successors of the pioneer settlers would hold land in this way. In some cases monasteries or other public institutions were granted land by the king. Hereditary heads of villages governing the affairs of the village were granted land, over which they exercised considerable rights, for their services. Another category of influential landholders were those who were allotted shares (*kaballi*) of a village or an estate or a tract of paddy fields. Such proprietors might have been the descendants of those older settlers of a village who had carved out large estates for themselves. There was a large group of officials to whom land was assigned in this way for their services. Any special meritorious service to the king was rewarded with grants of shares in villages. There also was the custom that where an individual, by his own enterprise, opened up waste land, he was granted tenurial rights over that land. The same applied to tanks and canals, in which there was considerable private ownership at the village level.

The bulk of the cultivators, who bore the brunt of the labor involved in cultivation, formed a class whose status was between that of freeholder and serf. Their relationship with the landlord was regulated by agreements of diverse forms, though their holdings were generally hereditary. The state had intervened in time to make their position more secure. They paid a share of the harvest to the lord, the size of which depended on such factors as the nature of the land, the crop grown, and the amenities supplied by the lord. A good number of the lords were absentees who leased the revenue from the land to a third party. Many of the tenants were settled on lands belonging to monasteries, where they had to deal with the officials of the monastery or with a middleman to whom the land had been leased. Whatever transaction the owner of the land may have entered into for the collection of his dues, it did not affect the tenant-cultivators because their rights were protected by the state as long as they fulfilled the conditions of their tenancy.

Of lower status than the tenant-cultivator was the serf (*dasun*). Serfs lived in separate villages and were paid in land for their services. They worked as laborers for the farmers and did other unskilled menial jobs in the village.

While the normal tax in the classical period was payment in cash or kind, there is also reference to obligatory service. Certain categories of peasants seem to have been obliged to perform a certain number of days' labor for the state. Such labor was utilized in works of a public character, especially the maintenance and construction of roads and irrigation tanks and channels. But service obligations were a minute aspect of the subject's dues to the state. In this period most of his dues were paid in cash or as a share of his produce.

There were several groups of highly specialized craftsmen in Sinhalese society. Their development was influenced by the hectic building activity of religious and secular edifices undertaken in the classic period. In medieval times the more skilled professionals had risen to a middle status between the highest agriculturalists and the lowest group of unskilled workers. The most important of these were the workers in the building trade, subdivided into carpenters, bricklayers, and workers in stone and in stucco. Details of their professional organization are lacking. It may be assumed that each group formed a guild on the south Indian model, and it was this guild which regulated conditions of service and trained its members. Stoneworkers would have been a highly skilled group because of the varied use of cut and polished stone in building. Dams and weirs, temples, palaces, fortification works were built in stone. The clipping of large slabs of stone from the rock surface and shaping them to requirement was an art in which they acquired special skill. Bricklayers were another significant group, for bricks were the most frequently used building material. The carpenters were also very important, for timber was used for the superstructures of large buildings, and ordinary houses were completely of wood.

The sculptor and the painter were two craftsmen very much in demand. Sculptors were required to make innumerable statues of the Buddha and of gods of the Hindu Pantheon. They also carved out beautiful figures on wall and rock surfaces. There remain some traces of the high quality of fresco painting of the time.

There were also the workers in metal: goldsmiths, coppersmiths, and blacksmiths. The last two would have been very numerous, as they supplied the large agricultural population with their tools and domestic implements. Those who worked in gold and silver provided the ornaments of which the Sinhalese even then were very fond. This artistic tradition has continued among the Sinhalese to modern times. All these crafts required special training, and hence the members of a guild held a position in society higher than that of the less skilled professions. Their work was of such a character that they were employed primarily by the state, and in return they were given lands which they leased out to cultivators, from whom they collected rent.

The lesser workers were those who satisfied the day-to-day needs of all classes of society. They included fishermen, potters, weavers, barbers, washermen. Fishermen operated in both inland waters and the open seas, for fish was an important item of diet. Potters were in great demand to supply the earthen vessels used in every home; they also made decorative pottery. Weavers worked in many different materials. There is evidence that the native weavers were supplemented by immigrants from south India, where the art of weaving was developed to great heights. Generally, it appears that a community would hire the services of individual members of these groups and pay them periodically in goods and sometimes cash. If craftsmen were employed by larger institutions such as a monastery or the royal court, they were assigned land in payment for their services.

The strategic location of the island, together with some of the coveted goods it produced, resulted in a fair degree of external trade from very early times. Situated midway between the two great civilizations of East and West, Ceylon was frequented by ships from both the Western and Eastern worlds. Ceylon came into the orbit of

Roman trade from the first century A.D. When, after the discovery of the monsoon and a direct sailing route across the Arabian Sea, Roman traders frequented the ports of southern India, they soon discovered the value of the island as well. Ceylon was known to nautical writers of the time as Taprobane, where pearls, precious stones, and ivory might be obtained. Mantota was the chief port of outlet in this period and continued so for a long time. Ptolemy's map reveals what was, for that time, a remarkable cartographical knowledge of Ceylon; though it does exaggerate the island's size, it is accurate on many points of detail. There is record of a Sinhalese embassy to the Roman emperor in the beginning of the first century A.D., which, though it did not achieve much because of linguistic difficulties, is proof of contact between them. Imports from the Mediterranean world included coral, fine earthenware, glass, and, no doubt, coins of gold and silver. Coral is mentioned as being used for decorating temples. With the decline of the Roman Empire in the third century A.D., this trade died out. Later, traders of the Middle East began to frequent Ceylonese ports. There is evidence of a colony of Nestorian Persians in the island, and after the eighth century the Arabs became the chief carriers of this trade.

Chinese traders also visited the ports of Ceylon, though it is not known that there was a regular traffic. Sinhalese embassies were sent to the Chinese court at various times from 400 to 700 A.D. Chinese coins and goods of Chinese origin have been uncovered in some of the ancient Sinhalese sites. After the tenth century traders from southeast Asia began to sail to Ceylon when the Sri Vijayan maritime empire was at the height of its power. There was a certain amount of direct trade with Ramanna, the southern Burmese kingdom, and Sinhalese traders used to call at Burmese ports. Trade with India was continuous and extensive. There were sailings from Ceylon to the port on the mouth of the Ganges and on the west to Surat. Horses were imported from north India. Trade connections with nearby southern India were the most intimate. Tamils managed a great proportion of the carrying trade of Ceylon. Throughout the classical period there were large colonies of Tamil traders in all parts of the island. Colonies of foreign merchants were settled in ports and in the capital, and the relations between them and the state officials were friendly. The names of some of the mercantile corporations show their Indian connections. The Sinhalese also participated in trade. Inscriptions refer to merchant guilds with chiefs called *setthis*. Under Parakrama Bahu I some measures were taken by the state to carry on trade directly. The development of a Sinhalese navy during his reign was related to these trading ventures.

Internal trade was not very extensive in an economy characterized by self-sufficient units. Circulation of coins was small and limited to the smaller denominations. Larger coins were mostly foreign and were intended for foreign trade. Internal trade took the form of supplying goods from one geographic region to another. Transport was mainly in carts drawn by bullocks. The country was well-provided with roads in ancient times, and trunk roads connected the four major regions and the chief ports. The bigger population centers had markets to which goods were brought and exchanged. Toll stations were erected by the state at different places and duties collected on certain goods in transit. Salt and the mining of precious stones were royal monopolies. Trade in the former was leased out to private people, but the latter seems to have been operated by the state. Proper government control was exercised on weights and measures used in the markets.

Developments in Buddhism; Buddhist Institutions and Learning

The history of the growth of Buddhism, its institutions, and its ideologies in the classical age of Sinhalese power forms a major chapter of Sinhalese history. The fortunes of Buddhism always provide a valuable index to the condition of Sinhalese civilization, and, judged by this index, the classical period is outstanding. With very few exceptions the Sinhalese people and their kings were practicing and believing Buddhists. From the time of its penetration to the island, Buddhism had been established as a state religion. Its institutions, sharing in the vicissitudes of the state, matured and flourished over the ages and were responsible for the permanence and strength of the religion. Among these the Sangha was crucial to the continuity of Buddhism in Ceylon. When the Sangha was "Ceylonized" by the admission of Sinhalese, it was thought to be a major step in establishing the religion. The Sangha was a community of individuals who had decided to give up worldly life and strive to achieve salvation by a life of meditation and service. On entry into the order the novitiate's head was shaven, and he donned the standard robes of the order, which in Ceylon were yellow. He took vows of celibacy and poverty. The novice had a period of training and education under his preceptor, after which he became a full-fledged *bhikkhu*. This was an important ceremonial occasion, known as the *upasampada*, and is comparable to an ordination. *Bhikkhus* of long experience and great erudition were entitled *thera* (elder) and *mahathera* (grand elder).

The regulations governing the Sangha are laid down in the Buddhist scriptures, but these are capable of different interpretations. There was no centralization of church organization in Buddhism, and different countries developed their own national traditions. Entering the order did not mean the total renunciation of worldly life for all time. An individual could take the vows and submit himself to the Sangha discipline for a period and then resume his normal vocation. This was a recognized practice in ancient Ceylon, especially among the upper classes and royalty. Instances exist of members of the royal family, even successors to the throne, becoming priests for a while. The individual would thus be instructed in the tenets of the faith and would have an opportunity to study and meditate upon the many religious texts under expert guidance. The discipline of mind and body was also held to give moral strength to face the problems that he would encounter in his secular life. This practice does not seem to have been as widespread as in Burma. It was by no means a normal custom among the upper classes, and it does not seem to have existed among the lower castes.

The monastery (*vihara*) was introduced into Ceylon with Buddhism. The first missionaries and their converts were settled in the Mahavihara on the outskirts of the capital city, which thus became the first monastery and the home of orthodoxy. Subsequently, several other monasteries arose around Anuradhapura and elsewhere. Besides the Mahavihara, three large monasteries were constructed before the fourth century A.D.—Mirisavati, Abhayagiri, and Jetavana.

The outer boundary of a monastery was marked out by a stone wall, and the property thus demarcated was holy and inviolable. It belonged communally to the Sangha. Within it were buildings of Buddhist worship. There was a *dagaba*, a semicircular mound enshrining a relic of the Buddha, a necessary structure in a monastery. Then there was a bo tree, centrally located, which was also an object of Buddhist worship. An image house contained one or more images of the Buddha. Some monasteries had preaching halls where the monks would deliver sermons to their congregations. And there were the dwellings of the *bhikkhus*. These were generally rows of cells, austerely built and furnished in keeping with the rigorous demands of the Sangha regulations. There was a central refectory from which the monks would procure their meals. A large monastery might house up to 5,000 monks.

From their inception, the monasteries were dependent on the state for their existence. According to the rules of the Sangha, its members lived on the charity of their congregation. But when the number of the Sangha increased, the monks could not depend on the uncertain favors of private charity. Even reliance on royal favor was shown to be dangerous, for royal power itself was uncertain. This was demonstrated in the first century B.C., when a severe famine and political instability left the monks in dire straits. To guard against a repetition of such calamities, later kings assigned independent sources of revenue to particular monasteries. The most common practice was to grant lands outright—paddy fields, gardens, or forests. As kings and wealthy citizens added to such grants, monasteries owned large temporalities by the medieval period. They became the biggest landowners in the country. Sometimes village tanks would be given to temples so that the revenues from the distribution of water would accrue to the monastery. Another method was to assign the revenues from villages or entire districts to a monastery. Slaves and serfs were assigned to them for labor. The rights of the state over monastic property was very limited. State officers could not enter them without permission, even to apprehend offenders. All of this involved the monastery in a great deal of secular administration. Tenant-cultivators on lands granted to the monastery became tenants of the monastery. The monastery had to collect rents from them and from the villages whose revenues had been assigned to it. For this it had to employ a large managerial staff of laymen. A large number of slaves

and laborers worked daily in a monastery attending to the menial
jobs, and their work had to be supervised and regulated. Thus, the
monastery was brought into contact with the life of the community
at several points, and as a result it increased its authority and influence over the community. It also secured a continuity and security
of its own interests and existence.

The church that showed such healthy growth in its institutions also
showed growth and change in its doctrines. The Buddhism that came
to Ceylon was of the primitive and orthodox form called Theravada.
It belonged to the broad philosophical system called Hinayana.
Briefly, this was a philosophy which held that the Buddhist *bhikkhu*,
by pursuing a career as a disciple of the Buddha, would attain Nirvana. An individual achieved salvation for himself by his own efforts.
Buddha was the Enlightened One who showed the way and had a
unique place in the system. These views represent those of the earliest
school of Buddhism in India. These were the views of the first missionaries, and thereafter it was this school that held sway in Ceylon
as approved orthodoxy. The Mahavihara fraternity adhered to this
school, and, as the oldest and most influential center of Buddhism
in Ceylon, it dominated the island's religious development. Most
of the smaller fraternities looked up to it. A majority of the kings associated themselves with the *vihara* and its school of Buddhism. So
great was this influence that generations of its *bhikkhu* scholars
looked upon the history of Buddhism in Ceylon essentially as the
history of the Mahavihara.

From about the second century B.C., new developments were taking place in Buddhist doctrine in India and were becoming quite
popular there. Mahayana Buddhism carried further some of the interpretations of the teachings of the Buddha. Aspects of these new
interpretations included the concept of the Bodhisattva, a superhu-
man being immediately below the Buddha who was worshipped by
the people, and a status to be achieved by pious adherents of the
faith. A Bodhisattva could help other people on the road to salvation, and to become one was thus a more altruistic ideal to strive for
than that of the achievement of Nirvana for oneself. The Buddha
himself was given a more deified status and placed into a cosmic
view that succeeding Buddhas were distributed through infinite space

and time. The concept of the Buddha thus approached that of the Brahman in Vedanta. A further step in the growth of Mahayanism was the introduction of image worship. Images of the Buddha and later of Bodhisattvas became increasingly popular. The scriptures of this school were mainly in Sanskrit, as opposed to Pali, the language of orthodoxy.

These ideas soon trickled into Ceylon to disturb the theological quiet of Sinhalese Buddhism. The first schism in the church of Ceylon took place in the first century B.C., when the monks of one of the larger *viharas*, the Abhayagiri, seceded from the Theravada sect and adopted the interpretations of a scholar called Dhammaruci. Thereafter Abhayagiri became virtually a center of rival heterodoxical sects moving away from the influence of the Mahavihara. In the third century A.D., a Mahayana sect called Vetullas came from India and flourished in the Abhayagiri *vihara*. These Mahayanist ideas were supported by some kings and consequently thrived. In the time of King Mahasena (276-303), Mahayanism was enthroned as the official religion, and the orthodox Mahavihara was suppressed. Its buildings were demolished and the material used for extension of the Abhayagiri. Mahavihara monks withdrew in hiding to the hill country. But their influence, especially among the nobility, was still so great that the king had to abandon his hostility to the Mahavihara. His sucessor made ample amends and restored all the privileges of the Mahavihara. A majority of the kings were patrons of the Mahavihara, and some of them took steps to suppress heterodoxical sects. In later years the Mahavihara did not dominate religious life as completely as it did at first. Every now and then, new sects representing some new interpretation of the canon would grow up. The Abhayagiri and the Jetavanarama *viharas* were the homes of such heterodoxical sects.

Under the influence of Mahayanist ideas, even the primitive Theravada changed its approach. These new ideas gradually seeped into the religious beliefs and forms of worship of the country under various guises. The worship of the Buddha image and of images of the Bodhisattvas, inaugurated in India under Mahayanist inspiration, soon extended to the island. The image house gradually became an important adjunct to the *vihara*. There was even some broadening in the Theravadin concept of the Buddha. A move was made toward admitting that some pious kings could become Buddhas in a future birth. This was probably to satisfy their royal patrons, to whom the Mahayanist ideal offered positive attractions. It appears that the tooth relic of the Buddha was brought to Ceylon in the fourth century A.D. under Mahayanist auspices. It was housed in the Abhayagiri, and the authorities of the Mahavihara had nothing to do with its worship.

Developments in the popular religion were largely unrelated to the schisms that took place in the Sangha. There was a clear shift of emphasis from the ethical to the devotional aspect of religion. Popular religion generally looks to symbols on which to concentrate its devotions, and these symbols become more important. Rituals and ceremonies were evolved to satisfy the lay Buddhist and became a vital part of lay worship. Listening to the preaching of the *dhamma* (doctrine) assumed the form of a festival. Large preaching halls were built in the *vihara*, and sometimes the sermon went on all night. The anniversary of the birth of the Buddha (Vesakh) was a festive occasion celebrated with state sponsorship. A considerable cult of relic worship grew up around relics of the Buddha and of the early disciples. The most popular of these was the worship of the tooth relic, which became the occasion for an important annual Buddhist ceremony. So important was this cult in the public mind that after some time the possession of the tooth relic became a necessary adjunct to the exercise of sovereignty by the monarch. Other relics of the Buddha in Ceylon were the collarbone, the hair, and the almsbowl.

The Sangha had a great influence on the Buddhist layman. There was a *vihara* in each village and town, and all members of the community betook themselves to the *vihara* for worship. Charity was a great ideal preached by Buddhism, and charity to the Sangha was specially recommended as giving great merit. Tradition records touching instances of solicitude and support for the clergy by the ordinary villagers. Though larger *viharas* were wealthy enough to look after themselves, in the smaller village temples the priests were dependent on the charity of the villagers. It was this association between the clergy and laity at the lowest levels of society, as much as the support of kings, that ensured the continuity of Buddhism among the Sinhalese. In the rare instances when kings ill-treated the Sangha, the people revolted against the king in support of the Sangha. This emphasis on charity also had the effect of influencing laymen to undertake works of social welfare. Wealthy people spent considerable sums putting up public works of one form or another. Furthermore, in a village community the *vihara* brought the different strata of that society together and was a unifying force among them. When pious kings took part in worship together with commoners, the leveling influence of Buddhism was seen in effect.

Among the people, there was a great deal of worship of other gods, deities, and spirits which Buddhism gradually absorbed. This was so strongly rooted among the people when they were converted that Buddhism had to come to terms with such practices. The deities of Upuluvan, Saman, and Natha were very popular among the people. There is dispute regarding the origin of these cults. Some authorities consider them to have been guardian deities of Ceylon, while others think that at least some are of Vedic origin. By the tenth century they had been given a place in Buddhist mythology. The belief in good and bad spirits was very common, and certain Buddhist rites were instituted to cater to it. A ceremony called *pirit* was evolved and performed by the *bhikkhus* to ward off evil spirits, especially in times of general calamity such as drought, epidemic, or famine. The ceremony consisted of the public recital of certain parts of the scriptures, the idea being that the power of the spirit of the Buddha would exorcise evil spirits from a place or a person. Unrecognized by official Buddhism, some kinds of magic art and sorcery were practiced which must have had their roots in pre-Aryan beliefs. There were specialists in the practice of these arts to whom the people resorted. If a person wanted to have some great desire fulfilled, or to avoid some impending calamity, or to win the support of some powerful personality, or to cause damage to his enemy, he would summon the professional magician to perform certain rites. This coexistence of the higher ideals of Buddhism with lower and more primitive religious elements was a feature of Sinhalese religion, lasting up to modern times.

Hindu Brahmanistic influences on Buddhism, already significant at the outset, continued to increase. There were at all times small colonies of Brahmins among the Sinhalese. Just as in India, some Brahmanical gods were recognized in Buddhism. It was thought that some favor could be won by worshipping these gods, and they themselves are represented as paying homage to the Buddha. Kings who patronized the official religion saw no obstacle to supporting Hindu temples and securing the performance of Brahmanical sacrifices as well. In the villages small Hindu shrines were located close to *viharas*. A Brahmin priest would be in attendance, and the local people would worship there. From the tenth century onward the influence of Hinduism on Buddhism seems to have been even greater than before. Kings are known to have constructed Hindu temples in the capital. Buddhist works of the period reveal a greater knowledge of Hindu mythology. There were also more disguised influences in forms of worship and ritual. The concept of devotion (*bhakti*) as a means to salvation, which became an important part of Hinduism from about the seventh century on, also influenced and entered Buddhism. The belief in the magical nature of incantations, a great Vedic phenomenon, became more and more common.

A major factor of this period was the intimate connection between the state and Buddhism. Royal power and the Buddhist hierarchy supported each other and derived strength from this support. Kings were great patrons of Buddhism partly because the influence of the Sangha made their thrones more secure. The Sangha supported royal power because the favor of royalty made the church affluent and influential. *Bhikkhus* had a great influence over the education of young princes, and when these princes sat on the throne they naturally looked to their teachers for advice. There is evidence that even on matters of state kings sought the advice of the higher dignitaries. *Bhikkhus* sometimes mediated between the king and his rebellious subjects or settled differences between members of the royal family. Just as kings had responsibilities toward the Sangha, they had also considerable rights over it. They could and did interfere in matters of dispute within the Sangha. When theological disputes took place, they would seek to maintain the unity of the Sangha by the exercise of their authority. A united and disciplined Sangha was of great importance to the state and would contribute to the moral well-being of their subjects. Whenever the clergy showed signs of decline in its standards of discipline and conduct, kings would step in and "purify" the Sangha. Many such instances of "purification" are recorded. Punishment for recalcitrant *bhikkhus* was promptly and severely administered, even to the extent of capital punishment.

Contacts of Sinhalese Buddhism with the rest of the Buddhist world were continuous. Sinhalese *bhikkhus* made pilgrimages to the holy places in India, visited the centers of Buddhism, and studied under famous teachers and philosophers in these institutions. In particular, there was contact with the two south Indian Buddhist centers of Nagarjunikonda and Kanchi. There is a very early record of a Sinhalese *vihara* at Nagarjunikonda in the Andhra district. The new heterodoxical sects of Ceylon were founded primarily by visiting theologians from India or by Sinhalese students of famous Indian philosophers. There were also occasional contacts with Chinese Buddhism. It appears that some Ceylonese nuns went to China in the fifth century A.D. and helped in the ordination of women there. In 411 A.D., the famous Chinese Buddhist traveler Fa Hsien visited Ceylon, stayed there for two years, and left fascinating impressions of Buddhism as practiced in Ceylon. With the Buddhist kingdoms of Southeast Asia, contacts were more intimate. Here the prevalent type of Buddhism was Theravada, as in Ceylon. There were frequent exchanges of pilgrims and scriptural knowledge with the Burmese kingdom of Ramanna. When, after the end of the Chola domination in the eleventh century, the Sinhalese monarch wanted to revitalize the Sangha, he sent envoys to the king of Upper Burma to send some duly ordained *bhikkhus*. These *bhikkhus* came to Ceylon, admitted new members to the order, and reconstituted the Sangha. From the twelfth century onward, with the almost complete disappearance of Buddhism from India, Ceylon looked more and more to Southeast Asia for its religious contacts. A Ceylonese monk seems to have had a share in the propagation of Buddhism in the Malayan kingdom of Ligor. Some years after Burma helped Ceylon re-establish the order of monks, Ceylon was able to offer Burma assistance in establishing orthodox Buddhism. A monk from Pagan came to Ceylon and took back with him some Sinhalese monks who established the Sinhalese Sangha in Burma. There seems to be some hint of relations with Cambodia, though these were not as intimate, as the Buddhism there was of the Mahayanist school. In the later medieval period, contacts with Burma and Siam were stronger than ever.

Buddhism was the agent of a flourishing literary activity among the Sinhalese. Pali, the language of Buddhism, found a comfortable home in Ceylon. It was studied in every monastery, and monks wrote prolifically in this language. A special contribution was the preservation of the Theravada canon in Pali after it was lost in India. Around it grew a body of writing in Pali and Sinhalese. A major landmark in the history of literature occurred when the canon was written down for the first time in the first century B.C. Up to this time it had been handed down orally, and there was the attendant danger that it might be lost. In the fifth century A.D., this canonical literature and the commentaries on it were brought together systematically by the great Indian scholars Buddhaghosa and Buddhadatta. Thereafter, original Pali literature was composed in Ceylon. In the twelfth century, subcommentaries were written to the classical commentaries of the canon, adding to the corpus of exegetical literature.

There exists a most remarkable tradition of historical literature among the Sinhalese, also under religious inspiration. The earliest examples of this literature are the *Dipavamsa* and the *Mahavamsa*. The latter was composed about the end of the fifth century A.D. by a *bhikkhu*. It deals with the lineage of kings from the semilegendary beginning of Sinhalese history up to the middle of the fourth century A.D. It was continued under the title *Chulavamsa* by another *bhikkhu*, Dhammakitti, in the thirteenth century, bringing the story up to the reign of Parakrama Bahu I. From here the history was taken up to the fourteenth century by another monkish author and concluded by yet another at the last stages of Sinhalese power in 1782. Thus the Sinhalese alone possess a continuous historical record from their earliest beginnings up to the loss of their independence. These works enable us to construct a successive lineage of Sinhalese kings with their regnal years, thereby giving a chronological and political framework to Sinhalese history. The synchronisms with events and personalities in India has made these works invaluable for a study of Indian history, and scholars have used the information contained in them to determine chronologies of Indian kings and empires.

Under the influence of Buddhism and Pali, the Sinhalese language was raised to a high standard. By the second century B.C., the language was being used for literary purposes. Thereafter, a body of religious writing explaining the Pali canon was accumulated in order to convey the ideas to those not acquainted with Pali. Translations of the original Pali texts also enriched the language. After the tenth century Sinhalese was further influenced by Sanskrit, and many Sanskritic words and idioms found their way into the language. Sinhalese writing of the twelfth and thirteenth centuries in particular shows a very high proportion of Sanskrit words.

Tamil influence on Sinhalese has always been considerable, in vocabulary, idiom, and grammatical structure. Partly because of the religious influence, the bulk of Sinhalese literature was scholastic, written by scholars for scholars, and followed set literary conventions. Poetry dominated the literature, and there was a tradition of folk poetry, much of which is lost to us. Some remarkable glimpses are seen in the verses inscribed on Sigiriya Rock, on the wall facing the fresco paintings of beautiful women. The paintings are of the fifth century A.D., but succeeding generations of visitors to this gallery have been moved to compose popular verses in Sinhalese and inscribe them on the walls.

Sanskrit was known and studied by the more scholarly monks. Most of the Mahayanist scriptures were in Sanskrit, and, with the spread of Mahayanism in Ceylon, Sanskrit took an important place in the curriculum of some of the *viharas*. Some of the more famous Sanskrit literary works were known. Treaties on polity and statecraft were read by kings. Sanskrit studies in Ceylon became more popular with the influence of the Pallavas, who were great patrons of Sanskrit. Sanskritic theories of poetics and rhetoric were studied keenly in Ceylon. There was some writing in Sanskrit, and there are some inscriptions in this language. Sinhalese poets sought to adhere closely to Sanskrit poetic models and produced works which are replicas of the Sanskrit original.

Formal education was imparted solely by monasteries. Children of the village were sent to the monastery to be tutored. The education of the ordinary folk would not have extended much beyond the stage of reading and writing at an elementary level. For higher education, one had to enter the Sangha, if only for a brief period. Later, further informal teaching in the monasteries developed into a formal institution known as the *pirivena*. The students were in residence and, when not being instructed, attended to the needs of the priest-teachers. It was similar in principle to the Hindu educational system, where the students lived with their teacher (*guru*) up to a certain age and then left to pursue their separate vocations. Education no doubt paid a great deal of attention to religion and secular subjects allied to religion. Thus, the three languages—Sinhalese, Pali, and Sanskrit—the religious texts, history, and logic from a Buddhist point of view would have been the chief subjects. Among other studies, astronomy, magic, and medicine are in evidence, especially medicine, in which Sinhalese practitioners achieved a high standard. The nature of learning was such as to develop most the power of memory at the expense of other faculties.

Achievements in the Fine Arts

In the fine arts the years up to the thirteenth century were the most creative in Sinhalese history. Sinhalese arts occupy a distinguished place in the heritage of Indian art and must be studied and understood as a part of this tradition. Like all Indian art, the Sinhalese was inspired and sustained over the centuries by religion. Together with the tenets of religion, the Sinhalese drew from India the early ideas of Buddhist art. Subsequently every major school of Indian art, whether Hindu or Buddhist, influenced the art of the Sinhalese. When these ideas entered Ceylon, they were cast into a different mold. Affected by the insular environment and a different religious and philosophical climate, these ideas were given a changed emphasis and a new outlook.

The creative talent of the Sinhalese expressed itself in almost all the known avenues of the fine arts. Some of these creations have withstood the ravages of time and man and have in recent times been restored to approximate the original as closely as possible. These rank with the great irrigation works mentioned above, and together they give the modern world an impression of the glories of Sinhalese civilization.

One of the earliest expressions of Sinhalese architecture was the *dagaba* or tumulus, the Sinhalese version of the Indian *stupa*, a mound-shaped structure embodying a Buddhist relic. The idea of the *stupa* came to Ceylon with Buddhism, but thereafter it was launched in a new and peculiar development unrelated to the Indian source. From the third century B.C., the Sinhalese developed the *dagaba* to great proportions. They learned to fashion the dome into six different shapes. On the summit of the dome, the conventional umbrella assumed different forms. Other embellishments were added to the *dagaba* which were absent in India, including projecting shrines, four in number, on the basal platform before the mound begins to rise. These later gave opportunities for lavish ornamentation and sculpture. It is said that the appearance of this feature in some Indian *stupas* was a result of Sinhalese influence. The domes were composed almost entirely of brick and were sometimes monumental in size, the largest one having a diameter of over 300 feet. Their construction must have been a task comparable to the pyramids of Egypt in magnitude, with some of which they compare in dimensions. A British engineer who saw them in their ruined state toward the end of the nineteenth century conjectured that the amount of brick used for one of them would have been sufficient to build a sizable town. When such a dome was plastered in white, as was the Ruanweli Dagaba, one can imagine the impression of grandeur it created, to be seen for miles in the surrounding country.

Another very impressive type of building was the image house, built of brick in varying shapes. Some of the most beautiful image houses were built in the twelfth and thirteenth centuries. They had tall, massive walls which rose from molded plinths and were decorated outside with architectural facades. The roofs were arched. The Thuparama, Lankatilaka, and Tivanka are three of the best examples. The circular shrines also achieved a high standard in the Polonnaruwa period. The Vatadage is the finest example of a circular shrine. Built in the twelfth century, it has been acclaimed as the most beautiful specimen of Buddhist stone architecture. It has concentric circular platforms and passages, with a round shrine in the center. Pillars have been skillfully used to emphasize the lines of this circular elevation. The four entrances have been embellished with ornamentation of great beauty. It is a great monument to the high standards of design and construction prevalent at that time.

Most of the secular buildings are clustered around Anuradhapura and Polonnaruwa, the two great capitals of the period, primarily in association with the royal palace. Those of the earlier phase at Anuradhapura are not very elaborate, though well planned. Especially worthy of notice are the royal pleasure gardens with their beautiful stone baths and ponds. At Polonnaruwa the palace was a more complex structure. The palace of Parakrama Bahu I seems to have had several stories. There were decorative pavilions in the precincts of the palace, and a bath designed in the shape of a lotus of eight petals.

An altogether distinct conception was the fortress and palace of Sigiriya, a very steep rock about 600 feet high on which a fifth-century Sinhalese king built his palace and capital. A combination of architectural and engineering genius transformed this inaccessible and unfriendly rock into one of the most beautiful of the ancient Sinhalese monuments. King Kasyapa was a parricide who lived in constant fear of the vengeance of his brother, who had fled to India. So the city was made perfectly defendable, with broad moats, earthen ramparts, and stone walls. A gallery, protected by a high wall, had steps of stone which led up to the overhanging and steep side of the rock. From there steps were cut out of the rock itself to begin a dangerous and steep ascent to the top. The entrance to these steps lay between the front legs of a carved lion, giving the impression that the whole rock was the body of a massive animal. On the top of the rock, the palace and gardens were beautifully laid out. The contours of the rock surface were used to plan a series of terraces as enclosed gardens, with a pavilion on the highest terrace. The whole conception showed boldness and originality of architectural ideas and the availability of immense resources in executing them. This monument has been intelligently restored and today attracts many foreign visitors.

In the art of stone sculpture there were some fascinating developments over the years, directly and perceptibly influenced by the various Indian schools. The earliest inspiration came from the

Buddhist Amaravati school in Andhra, which flourished from the second century B.C. Early sculpture was in the form of bas-reliefs to *stupas*, carvings on rock surfaces, and images. The Buddha image is the most exciting of the creations of Sinhalese sculpture, and we see it in diverse forms in succeeding periods. Here, too, the Amaravati influence seems to be evident in the earliest phase. Some isolated attempts have been made by modern Sinhalese scholars to postulate a Sinhalese origin to the Buddha image.* But these attempts are as yet unconvincing, and we must continue with the generally accepted view that the free-standing Buddha was introduced to Ceylon from Andhra. From about the second century A.D., colossal images in the round were being made out of limestone and out of natural rock. The Buddhas were of standing, sitting, or recumbent postures. The images of the earlier phase were heavy and somewhat rigid in their pose. But by the fourth century A.D., the Sinhalese were beginning to make statues of exquisite charm and were able to capture some depth of feeling in the facial expressions they gave to the Buddha. The Sinhalese Buddhas were strong, solid figures, reflecting enormous power and determination. In contrast with some Indian types, never was the voluptuousness of bodily beauty or the suggestion of a heavenly, otherworldly being allowed to intrude into the statue. One of these, a seated Buddha located in a grove near the *vihara* of Abhayagiri, is held to be among the best statues in any part of the Buddhist world. Gupta influences can be seen in the imagery of Ceylon of this period. After the capital shifted to Polonnaruwa, new achievements were made. Innumerable images were made to be housed in the several shrine rooms that had been built. The images in the Galvihara were colossal—a recumbent Buddha 50 feet in length and a standing Buddha 25 feet high. There is another huge figure, unidentified, carved from a large boulder in Polonnaruwa. It seems to be the image of a king, some say Parakrama Bahu I, and the sculptor has given to it nobility and a lifelike quality.

* D. T. Devendra, *Classical Sinhalese Sculpture* (London: 1958), pp. 13-15; Siri Gunasinghe, "A Sinhalese Contribution to the Development of the Buddha Image," *Ceylon Journal of Historical and Social Studies*, Vol. III, No. 1 (January-June, 1960), pp. 59-72.

Sculptural embellishments to architecture developed to great proportions as an art in itself. Flights of steps at entrances to buildings, pillars and colonnades, and walls were decorated with beautiful carvings based on mythology. Figures of dwarfs, animals, humans, birds, and flowers were intricately carved. One of the most popular embellishments was the guardstone, carved with the figure of a *naga* in human form performing guard duties for the building. These adorn almost all buildings throughout the period, and some of them are exquisite works of art. Another piece of ornamentation is the moonstone, shaped in the form of a half moon, at building entrances, with carvings of floral designs, birds, and animals in concentric bands. All of these convey a feeling of mystic symbolism appropriate to the buildings which they adorn. The sculpture on open rock face is strongly influenced by Pallava style. The Pallavas of Kanchi achieved great heights in carving on natural rocks and boulders, and their epic sculpture on the rock at Mamallapuram has been held as the supreme example of this art. Some sculpture in Anuradhapura may be taken almost as copies of the Pallava work. This Pallava influence characterized Sinhalese carving of animals, birds, and human figures for a long time.

The art of painting, too, developed early, though contemporary visual evidence of this is not as plentiful as of the other arts. Most of the painting seems to have been destroyed by natural causes. There is evidence that religious edifices had decorative painting on the walls. One substantial relic of fresco painting has fortunately come down to us, and from it we can form some judgment of the high standards achieved. In the rock capital of Sigiriya, which the king decorated with paintings, one portion is now in a good state of preservation thanks to the natural shelter of an overhanging ledge. These paintings show celestial women, singly and in pairs, toying with flowers. The concept of beauty conforms to the classical Indian type: slender waists, large breasts, long, slim arms, and tapering fingers. But the faces show individual character and probably reflect actual Sinhalese types. The jewelery and coiffures worn by the women still inspire fashions among modern Sinhalese ladies. The drawings were entirely freehand, and the colors have remained fresh after 1,500 years. Other fragments of paintings are available in scattered temples. Some examples of the twelfth and thirteen century show that the art was still alive, though deteriorating in quality.

The casting of metal images, mainly in bronze, was a sphere in which considerable distinction was achieved. From the fifth to twelfth centuries various examples have come down to us. There are a number of Buddha images in bronze, some of which are of high quality. Some images of the Buddha are of Mahayanist inspiration, as are those of Bodhisattvas found in Ceylon. Gupta influences are evident in many of these pieces. Bronzeworkers also produced lamps artistically adorned with figures. Bronze statues were sometimes replicas of stone figures and were deposited in relic chambers. Some of the figures show Hindu influence; statues of Hindu gods were cast and buried under the shrines. Most of these images are of mediocre quality, but some outstanding specimens show the talent at its best.

DECLINE AND DECADENCE, A.D. 1200–1500

The history of Sinhalese civilization enters a distinct new phase with the beginning of the thirteenth century. At that time certain radical changes took place in Sinhalese political fortunes, with consequences that sharply distinguish the subsequent years from the classical period. These may be said to be features of decline, a decline that gathered momentum and eventually led to the loss of independence.

Parakrama Bahu I was the last of the great Sinhalese kings. A period of 50 years after his death produced 14 rulers at Polonnaruwa, most of them weaklings. The policy of dynastic marriages with Indian royal families had resulted in factionalism in court. The influence of these foreign factions was increasing, at the cost of Sinhalese power. The most powerful of the factions was that of the Kalingas, a dynasty of eastern India with which Sinhalese kings had periodically established nuptial connections. (There has been a recent attempt to locate Kalinga in the Malay peninsula and thus give a revolutionary interpretation to subsequent Sinhalese history, but the case must still be regarded as not proven.*) After Parakrama Bahui the throne passed to the Kalinga dynasty, which maintained a

* C. W. Nicholas and S. Paranavitana, A *Concise History of Ceylon* (Colombo: 1961), pp. 236-46.

shaky hold at Polonnaruwa for five decades. Its claims were contested by a Pandyan faction, which also had had connections with Sinhalese royalty, besides its ties with the ancient Pandyan dynasty in south India that was now reasserting itself after a period of subjection to the Cholas. To add to the confusion, Chola invasions of Ceylon that had been suspended when the Sinhalese kingdom strengthened itself in the twelfth century were now resumed. Mercenary armies of various races, mainly from southern India, swept overland and formed the base of the power of non-Sinhalese factions. Internecine conflicts among these factions were a common occurrence. The culmination of all these misfortunes was the reign of the last king of the Kalinga dynasty, Magha (1215-36), who adopted a policy of blood and terror to maintain his throne. Sinhalese tradition remembers his rule as a dark period which completely undermined the social and religious organization of the country.

While political dissension and weakness seized the Polonnaruwa kingdom, other centers of Sinhalese power rose in the outlying parts. Local rulers of Ruhuna in the southeast and Mayarata in the southwest set up their own authorities and resisted the claims of the central government which had fallen into foreign and incompetent hands. As authority at Polonnaruwa declined, some of these provincial centers rose to strong positions, and their rulers laid claim to sovereignty. After the death of Magha the ruler at Dambadeniya, 75 miles southwest of Polonnaruwa, became the dominant Sinhalese power, and the capital shifted to this small city. This began the shifting of capitals southward and southwestward. The rulers selected their capitals with consideration to defense and to their own parochial sources of power. In chronological sequence, the capitals of the subsequent years were Kurunegala, Gampola, Rayigama, and Kotte. When the first Portuguese fleet was blown into Colombo harbor in 1505, the Kotte kingdom was the major Sinhalese dynasty. In the course of two and a half centuries, Sinhalese political power moved far from its traditional homelands of Rajaratta, where it had previously maintained itself for a millennium and a half.

This drift in the seat of political authority toward the southwest was both the cause and consequence of some interesting political developments in the north. One major event of these times was that the Sinhalese kingdom lost its monopoly of political power in Ceylon. After the middle of the thirteenth century there arose in the northern part of the island a separate kingdom ruled by a south Indian Tamil dynasty. The withdrawal of Sinhalese power from the north was utilized by this dynasty to entrench itself, and it became a permanent feature in the later medieval political history of Ceylon. There were constant conflicts between the Tamil kingdom and the Sinhalese rulers as the Tamils pushed their frontiers southward. Though for a brief period this kingdom was subjugated by Parakrama Bahu VI of Kotte, it soon regained its independence and kept it until the arrival of the Portuguese. Even over their own dominions in the southern part of the country, the hold of Sinhalese kings was not supreme. There was more than one center of power, and the king at some times was not much more than first among equals. Military chiefs set themselves up in various parts of the country and owed but a nominal allegiance to the crowned head.

Foreign invasions were another of the troubles of the Sinhalese kingdom. Political weakness attracted invasions from south India. In the second half of the thirteenth century there were frequent Pandyan invasions, and at one time they even took away the tooth relic, sacred symbol of Sinhalese sovereignty. At about the same time there were two invasions by a ruler of the Malay peninsula, Chandrabhanu. He seems to have been after the tooth relic, the possession of which, as a Buddhist, he would have valued. These invasions were repulsed by the Sinhalese with Pandyan help. The Pandyan kingdom centered at Madura was annihilated by the Islamic invasion of the far south in 1334. But the consolidation of Dravidian lands under the Vijayanagar empire that took place soon after called into existence a strong power in this region that influenced the politics of Ceylon. Vijayanagar records mention many invasions of Ceylon in the first half of the fifteenth century and generally speak of Ceylon as part of their imperial domains. But it is not known how far their authority extended, and it seems likely that their invasions and victories were over the Tamil kingdom and that they did not penetrate southward to the seat of Sinhalese power.

Another interesting external invasion that influenced the politics

of Ceylon came from China. The third emperor of the Ming dynasty
fitted out some expeditions under the great Admiral Cheng Ho as
part of a policy of expanding Chinese power into the Indian Ocean.
In one of these expeditions (1405-7), which took him to the major
ports of the Indian Ocean, Cheng Ho landed in Ceylon. At that
time the Sinhalese ruler was Bhuvaneka Bahu V, but the effective
authority was Vira Alakesvara. The resistance offered by him made
Cheng Ho retreat hastily, but he returned in 1411. Again Vira
Alakesvara opposed the Chinese but was defeated and taken captive,
together with some of his ministers and the tooth relic. Later they
were released, and the Sinhalese notables with Chinese help set up
Parakrama Bahu VI on the throne. This king rose to become the
most powerful Sinhalese ruler of the period.

Consequent on this general decline of political power was the decay of a whole civilization. These years witnessed the deterioration
of the very productive and prosperous tank system, which had sustained a vigorous population and paved the way for high artistic
achievements. The construction and maintenance of the large irrigation works and the monumental religious edifices had been made
possible by a wealthy state. The state in turn was made powerful by
a prosperous agricultural economy and an ostentatious patronage of
religion. Each was dependent on the other. Now the decline of royal
power, one major link in this chain, led to the collapse of everything
else linked to it. When kings started to shift their residences and
capitals from considerations of personal safety, taking with them
the entire central administrative machinery, the population itself
gradually shifted in the direction of the new capital. Understandably,
this was a slow process, because the ordinary people could not up-
root themselves as easily as the royal entourage. At first it was the
nobility and their retainers who followed the kings, and the shifting
of population in mass took place locally within the northern and
north-central regions. Later on, with the collapse of one network of
tanks after the other, there took place a more drastic depopulation
of the entire ancient region. By the beginning of the period of European penetration, early European observers were able to report the
collapse of a once flourishing civilization and note that the centers
of Sinhalese population were now the south, southwest, and central

highlands. Corresponding changes in agricultural techniques and land systems also took place.

A combination of factors reacting on each other had brought about this phenomenal collapse. For a long time it seemed an easy solution for historians to point to the Dravidian invasions, the Chola occupation (1017-70), and the ravages of the Kalinga kings as the sole explanation. It is now recognized, however, that these are not sufficient and that one has to look deeper into the social structure and economic organization. The invasions were, no doubt, factors that exposed the weaknesses of Sinhalese political power, but there is evidence that they were not the exclusive agents of destruction. In earlier times the Sinhalese kingdom had been able to rise again after temporary setbacks, but that it could not do so now points to some inherent weakness. The rule of the foreign Kalinga kings was the more unfortunate, because, at a time when the state ought to have stepped in to remedy the ill effects of foreign invasions, these kings had neither the ability nor the inclination to do so. The fact that, even at this time, the Sinhalese dynasty could not throw up men of stature to reassert political leadership shows that the natural causes of decay of a long lineage of kings had set in.

Some of the seeds of subsequent decline had been sown in the period of greatness. The twelfth century was in many respects the apex of Sinhalese glory. At this time the Sinhalese had been more than an insular power. Under Parakrama Bahu I they participated vigorously in south Indian and Southeast Asian politics. We have noted their artistic and technical achievements; yet the magnitude and splendor of these works consumed a great deal of the state's resources. Foreign wars drained the treasury without bringing any tangible benefits in return. The great religious edifices were economically wasteful, and the construction of so many of these in such a short time must have strained the economy. The patronage of religion by the state had become a great burden, as religious institutions had grown enormously. There is evidence that the incidence of taxation was rather heavy at this time. The governmental machinery itself was overcentralized under Parakrama Bahu. This was a burden which subsequent kings had to carry but for which they lacked the ability. Parakrama Bahu I thus bequeathed to his successors a tradition of excessive state expenditure and a cumbersome centralized administration. A period of economy and cautious spending would have been necessary to recuperate, but conditions did not permit such a policy.

The elaborate system of irrigation on which the country's agriculture depended necessitated a bureaucracy both in the center and at the village level. This bureaucracy was drawn from the landed gentry, the traditional leaders in society. They were the ministers at the capital and the superintendents of irrigation and agriculture in the villages. With the Kalinga dynasty the power and position of the Sinhalese nobility declined. These kings tended to rely on their compatriots to fill the higher roles in the administration. In fact, the richer members of Sinhalese society were subject to plunder and pillaging by these foreign officials. The Kalinga kingdom had a quasi-military form of government. Bodies of mercenary troops were scattered about the country to keep law and order, and military leaders undertook many administrative functions, superseding the traditional gentry. Besides, members of the gentry found it politic to withdraw to the courts of Sinhalese leaders who had set themselves up elsewhere. Thus, the traditional methods for the upkeep of the agricultural and irrigation systems broke down. The military overlords were not interested in attending to this onerous task. The irrigation system had to be kept in constant repair; silting, which would lead to major breaches had to be continuously guarded against. One by one many of the larger tanks were breached, owing to neglect, and large tracts of land lost their supply of water. There also was a certain amount of deliberate destruction by rival factions struggling for power. When the irrigation system broke down, it was obvious that the dry zone could not sustain a population as dense as before. Hence the movement toward areas of greater rainfall. Jungle spreads fast into lands left uncultivated for even a short time. A brief period of neglect was therefore bound to do permanent damage to the agricultural system.

Other hypotheses are advanced to explain the Sinhalese decline. In certain areas the same land had been cultivated in much the same fashion for centuries. Would this have led to exhaustion of the fertility of the soil? This factor would have caused the depopulation of some regions, or at least a lessening of the capacity of the land to support the existing population. The spread of malaria in the dry zone may also have been a factor, though in the latter part of the period of decline. It is noteworthy that, when attempts were first made in the twentieth century to revive agriculture in the dry zone, malaria was found to be the main obstacle. It had left the people inert and febrile and caused a very high death rate. British administrators found that all the aforementioned factors had operated cumulatively for a long period, leaving behind the skeletal remains of a once prosperous economy.

In the three centuries (thirteenth-sixteenth) that may be termed a period of decline, Sinhalese civilization changed drastically. Rice cultivation was still an important activity in the new population centers of the south and southwest, but techniques of cultivation had to be changed to suit the undulating lands and the different type of soil. Land suitable for rice was not so extensive as before, and other grains had to be cultivated as supplements. Irrigation was undertaken, but, because of the different terrain, the technique had to be different, and the works were all of moderate proportions. Garden produce such as coconut and jack fruit were important elements in the diet of the people. It was at this time, too, that the growing of spices for export became a major economic function. In the absence of sufficient rice, the people had to make do with various substitute grains and jams. Cattle breeding became less popular and milk foods less common, so that the nutritive value of the diet declined. The debasement of coinage was an index to the general economic decline. Coins which in the period of prosperity were either of gold or silver were now almost exclusively of copper. Less money was in circulation, and this affected the nature of payment of tax obligations.

Trade took a more important place in the country's economy. This is one of the reasons for the shift of the capitals toward the coast so that kings might better control trade. Many of the articles of trade were royal monopolies and thus an important source of state revenue. Trade was concentrated on the southwestern coast, where many new ports rose to prominence. Almost all the traders were foreigners, who settled in colonies on the seacoast. In the fourteenth century cinnamon first became an important article of the export trade, thus beginning an epic which shaped the course of the island's history, for the cinnamon of Ceylon which the Arab traders supplied to the world attracted many others who wanted to find it for themselves. Colombo and Galle became important ports to handle this trade, situated as they were in the heart of the country where cinnamon and other spices grew. The trade of the northern ports, handling different commodities, was outside the control of the Sinhalese. In 1283 the Sinhalese king, Bhuvaneka Bahu I, sent an embassy to the sultan of Egypt to seek a commercial agreement. But commerce was of such a kind as not to involve the people. The king was the monopolist of many of the articles, and he entered into contracts with foreign traders or leased the harbor to them for revenue.

Some very significant changes took place in land holding relations. In place of the earlier grain tax payable directly to the state in cash or in kind, there now grew up a system of service tenure. The majority of land was now held on the basis of service, and the grain tax had virtually disappeared by the seventeenth century. Some taxes which earlier were paid to the state were now collected by the village headman. The kings could no longer maintain a specialized administration for the assessment and collection of revenue, and so they extended tenancy by service. Tithe-paying lands and service lands were gradually merged. No large surplus accrued to the state. This was one of the reasons why kings vigorously tapped foreign trade as the only important source of wealth.

The weakening of state power was reflected in a general impoverishment of Buddhist institutions. The great monasteries of Anuradhapura and Polonnaruwa were disbanded, and small centers were established in or near the new capitals. No doubt kings continued with their functions as patrons of the faith, such as they could in the troubled times. The frequent purges of the Sangha instituted by them show the indiscipline and decadence of the Buddhist clergy. The doctrinal differences of an earlier era were forgotten, and Theravada, having absorbed some of the Mahayanist ideas and rituals, monopolized Ceylonese Buddhism. Ties with Burma and Siam, the homes of Theravada Buddhism, were even closer in this period. Frequent missions were exchanged with both these countries. There was an even greater penetration of Hindu ideas in Buddhist worship in this period, largely because of greater physical contact with the Tamils. This influence is seen in many fields. Many of the Dravidian loan-words and idioms in the Sinhalese language are probably of this period, because of the intensive contact between the two people at this time. There was a good deal of writing in Sinhalese in this period, especially in the medium of prose, but the art of the period is only a pale reflection of the classical greatness. As the kings shifted to new capitals, they constructed new edifices, but not of a size or grandeur comparable to the earlier ones. Dravidian styles in temple building were adopted in the latter part of the period. The sculptures are frigid copies of the classical models. Some of the artistic traditions were preserved until modern times as folk art in the central highlands, where attempts are now being made to revive them once again.

97

THREE

THE TAMILS OF CEYLON

The people who speak the Tamil language belong to a group whose origins are in dispute. Tamil belongs to the Dravidian group of languages and is, in fact, the oldest literary language of this group. The people who speak Dravidian languages are concentrated in the southern part of peninsular India, where they have an old recorded history. Some hold that they are a people indigenous to India, the whole of which they once occupied before being driven southward by the invading Aryans. Still others have put forward the hypothesis that the Dravidians were a people who immigrated into India from the Mediterranean regions in prehistoric times and were responsible for the Indus valley culture. The invading Aryans destroyed this culture and drove them southward. According to a third view, the Dravidians came to India after the Aryans and occupied the southern regions into which the Aryans had not spread. Whatever their origins, by the third century B.C. there were well-established Tamil kingdoms in the south. Soon after, the Tamil language developed forms of expression of a high standard. The earliest extant literature in this language is from the first century B.C., known as the Sangam period. Tamil civilization at that time was an urban civilization with a flourishing trade with the Western world and high artistic achievements. The Tamil homelands corresponded to what are today the states of Madras and Kerala, thus the eastern and western coasts of the southern tip of India. These lands saw the rise and fall of several Tamil kingdoms and empires until the British conquered the whole subcontinent.

Geologically, Ceylon is a part of peninsular India. They both stand on the same continental shelf. The sea that separates the two land masses came into existence, geologically speaking, in recent times and is only about 15 fathoms in depth at the narrowest parts, where the distance is 30 to 50 miles. The island of Ceylon and its products were very well known, according to the earliest Tamil literature. Mantota, a port situated on the Ceylon side of the straits, was referred to and must have been a frequent port of call of Tamil traders. As the history of both regions in the pre-Sinhalese period is still the subject of speculation, nothing specific can be said regarding contact between them. Archaeological work in some megalithic remains in the Deccan and far south is throwing new light on the spread of what may be the early Dravidian peoples into southern India in the first millennium B.C. Urn burials found in a site north of Puttalam seem to be similar to those found at Adichchanallur in Tamil Nad. Could this megalithic parent of the later Dravidian civilization have spread to Ceylon, and could this have been the culture that existed in Ceylon when the Aryans landed there?

Whether this be so or not, there is no doubt that at the time of Aryan colonization of Ceylon the inhabitants of the Tamil country played an important role in the establishment of this civilization. This historical fact is recorded in Sinhalese tradition in many ways. The legendary hero Vijaya found brides for himself and his followers in the Pandyan kingdom. Artisan families came from there to serve as craftsmen. A few centuries later there is more definite evidence of the presence and, indeed, the increasing influence of the Tamils. In the third century B.C. two Tamils described as horse traders were able to seize the throne from the Sinhalese royal line and hold power for a period of 22 years. Yet another Tamil, Elara, said to be of the Chola line, seized and held power at Anuradhapura for 44 years. He was defeated by the Sinhalese ruler Duttugemunu, who re-established the Sinhalese lineage. The Buddhist chroniclers emphasize that all these Tamil rulers governed the country righteously. That they continued state patronage of Buddhism is shown by epigraphic evidence. Elara in particular gained a legendary reputation in Sinhalese tradition for his sense of justice. It appears that the portrayal of the conflict between Elara and Duttugemunu as a racial war between Tamils and Sinhalese is a later interpretation. Reading the account carefully, one sees it more as a dynastic battle, purely political in its nature. Many Sinhalese generals fought on the side of Elara. If he had been purely a foreign usurper who forced his way onto the throne, he could not have held power so long nor put up such a hard fight when attacked by his Sinhalese adversary. There is other evidence for the existence of large Tamil colonies in the harbors and in the capital city in the early period. A Tamil householder's terrace has been discovered in Anuradhapura, with inscriptions labeling the seats of the members. The seat of honor is that of a ship captain, which shows that the colony must have been predominantly a commercial one.

In the first century B.C., power passed again into the hands of Tamil rulers for about 14 years (102-89). They are described as a group of seven Tamil chiefs, probably of Pandyan extraction, who landed at the port of Mantota with a large army. They advanced to the capital and defeated the reigning king, Vattagamani, who fled to the hill country. Five of the chiefs stayed behind to rule the kingdom and were later dislodged by Vattagamani, who returned from exile to the throne. It was again from the Pandyan dynasty that the next Tamil rulers of Ceylon were drawn four centuries later. As a result of a successful invasion in the fifth century A.D., six Tamil rulers ruled at Anuradhapura for about 26 years. Their rule is seen to have extended to the southernmost parts of the island. These rulers also patronized Buddhism, and there are records of donations they made to monasteries. They were overthrown by Dhatusena, another hero in Sinhalese tradition. It was at this time that the *Mahavamsa* was written. It was at this time also that an anti-Tamil feeling entered Sinhalese nationalism, probably the result of this quarter of a century of Pandyan power, and probably restricted to the clergy.

In the first millennium of Sinhalese colonization of Ceylon, Tamil influence was thus felt in successive waves. There were two types of immigrations: the peaceful settlers and the invaders. The invaders do not seem to have come as permanent colonists and not in large number. The settlers came to perform diverse functions. Sinhalese kings used to marry into Tamil royal families. The royal brides and their retinues were absorbed into Sinhalese culture. Colonies of merchants did not plant themselves permanently at one place and therefore did not leave an impact on the country. Small groups of craftsmen settled in Sinhalese villages in a predominantly Sinhalese population and were assimilated. There is evidence that some Sinhalese castes originated in this manner. An ever-increasing number of mercenary soldiers were brought from south India by the Sinhalese kings. These people lived in their own cantonments with little or no contact with the Sinhalese. Here they continued practicing their own ways of life, language, and religion. Yet, from the seventh century onward, they were a powerful force in the country, interfering in the dynastic struggles of the Sinhalese and helping to put in power kings favorable to their own interests. Their leaders were appointed to high offices in the state. The first temporary shift of the capital from Anuradhapura was caused by the desire of the ruling monarch to rid himself of Tamil political influence. From this time, accentuated by growing contact between the Sinhalese and the Tamil kingdoms of south India, Tamil influence on Sinhalese governmental organization was greater than ever. This was particularly so in the sphere of land tenure and taxation, where terms of south Indian origin now made their appearance and were increasingly in vogue thereafter. Titles of officers that are of Tamil origin were also in evidence. Some of these terms are still in existence.

Hindu temples belonging to this early period which are scattered in many parts of the country attest to the presence of Tamil settler communities. There are three Siva temples of great antiquity, and these enable us to make reasonable inferences regarding Tamil settlements in the early centuries of the Christian era. Thirukethisvaram at Mantota and Konesvaram at Trincomalee are mentioned in early Tamil literature as famous Saiva centers which attracted pilgrims from south India. Thirukovil, a few miles south of Batticaloa, seems also to be a temple of the early period. These three places may thus be taken to be the seats of the oldest Tamil colonies of people engaged in trade, agriculture, and fishing. The coastal areas of the Jaffna peninsula, too, seem to have been colonized, particularly the ports at which small boats could call. There is indication of a sixth-century movement from Jaffna along the coast to Batticaloa. By the tenth century, the first stage of Tamil settlements was complete. Research on the laws of the Ceylon Tamil peoples seems to indicate that most of the settlers of this early stage came from the Malabar coast. This is understandable, as trading and migrating movements were in evidence from very early times among the peoples of this coast. They seem to have handed down to succeeding colonists some of the elements of their early social structure. The people of Malabar, from whom these early immigrants were drawn, broke away from the mainstream of the Tamil language by evolving a separate language for themselves (Malayalam) from the twelfth century onward. This left the Malabar settlers of Ceylon as a Tamil-speaking people with a social organization different from that of the other Tamil communities of a reduced Tamil Nad.

The next period of Tamil rule of Ceylon was the Chola occupation. The nature of their rule differed from earlier ones. Each of the earlier conquests had been attempted by an indigenous Tamil, or by an adventurer from the mainland who settled down and ruled the country for as long as he could. In the case of the Chola conquest, the first (and the last) attempt was made to rule the country as part of an Indian empire. Under Rajaraja I, an able administrator, Ceylon was organized as a province of the Chola empire, and it remained so until 1070, when the Cholas were expelled. Sinhalese chronicles paint the Chola period in lurid color, but the fragmentary evidence available does not support this. There was naturally some destruction of property in the course of the fighting that was so frequent in this period, but there was no deliberate spoliation of Buddhist shrines. There is at least one evidence of a donation to a Buddhist shrine, and it may be assumed that the Cholas, in keeping with contemporary practice, were tolerant of Buddhism. No doubt, Hinduism and Tamil interests received a boost under the Cholas. It is known that the Tamils who were settled in the capital supported the Cholas in their fight against the Sinhalese kings. A number of Siva and Vishnu temples were built, one beautiful structure in the Chola style of the period at Polonnaruwa being noteworthy. We may also assume that there were many new Tamil settlers taking advantage of the Chola occupation, thus adding to the Tamil element in the population of north Ceylon. There was certainly an influx of Brahmins at this time, and their function must have been to cater to the growing Hindu community. Some of the best specimens of Chola bronzes have been unearthed in Ceylon. Thus, there is every evidence that Chola occupation was a great fillip to Saivite Hinduism in Ceylon.

The overthrow of the Cholas and reassertion of Sinhalese power did not mean the extermination of Tamil influence. The increase in numbers of the Tamil community, their general affluence, and the influential positions they held in the militia and administration made this impossible. Indeed, Sinhalese royalty was intermixed with Tamil blood and Buddhism penetrated by Hindu influence. Parakrama Bahu I, the great architect of Sinhalese revival, was the grandson of a Pandyan prince. Tamil and Kalinga queens were numerous, and Tamil and Kannada mercenaries were widely used. The enthronement of the Kalinga dynasty was beneficial to the interests of the Tamils. They were Hindus and were closely connected in India with the Cholas by marriage. The activities of the Kalinga ruler Magha were partly responsible for the weakening of Sinhalese power in northern Ceylon and thus indirectly helped the establishment of an independent Tamil kingdom there.

The establishment of an independent Tamil kingdom in Ceylon in the thirteenth century is a landmark in the history of the Ceylon Tamils. No doubt it was helped by the weakness of Sinhalese political power. But it was also the culmination of centuries of expanding Tamil interests and elements in Ceylonese society. In the early years, small, isolated immigrant groups had been absorbed into the body of Sinhalese society. More intensive migration in the middle of the first millennium A.D. resulted in concentrations of Tamils in particular geographic localities. Because of the nearness to the Tamil coast, they tended to cluster in northern Ceylon, where thus, in place of a homogeneous Sinhalese population, if ever there had been one, there now grew two major communal groups. The coming of the Tamils in large numbers enabled them to maintain their identity as a language-culture group. By the thirteenth century, this group had become so strong that they could easily take advantage of Sinhalese weakness to set up an independent political authority. The details of the origin of this kingdom are obscure and still the subject of controversy. There is a school which antedates the formation of this kingdom and holds that there was a Tamil kingdom in Jaffna centuries earlier, at the time of the classical Sinhalese kingdom. The state of Tamil studies in Ceylon, in particular the almost complete absence of any archaeological work in the Jaffna peninsula, does not help us to confirm or reject this hypothesis. What we can say with certainty is that by 1325 the Tamil kingdom had come onto the historical scene.

The kingdom was founded by a line of kings who called themselves Arya Chakravartis. Tamil tradition has it that the founders came from Ramesvaram, an island at the southernmost tip of India. This family had immigrated to Ramesvaram from the Kalinga region and were a branch of the Ganga dynasty. They seem to have married into Brahmin families of Ramesvaram and taken the title *Arya*, probably to denote this intermixture with the highest Aryan caste. We do not know definitely who the first Arya ruler of Jaffna was. Jayabahu, who is referred to as ruler of the north while Magha was ruler at Polonnaruwa, was probably the founder of the line, and it is likely that he was some relation of Magha, who was also a scion of the Ganga dynasty. Thereafter came a succession of Arya Chakravartis who ruled from Nallur. The kingdom of Jaffna, known thus because the center of its power was the Jaffna peninsula, now began a separate existence as one of the political entities on the island and entered the struggles with other kingdoms for political power. Though its political boundaries shifted with its changing fortunes, it generally embraced the limits occupied by the Tamil-speaking people. Within a few years of its establishment, cultural dividing lines and political frontiers almost coincided.

Fortunately for the Tamil kingdom in the half century after its foundation, the Sinhalese were ruled by the weak kings of the Dambadeniya dynasty. Internecine disputes among these kings and the destruction of Rajarata created a no man's land between the two kingdoms behind which the new state could consolidate itself. The frequent Pandyan invasions exhausted whatever was left of Sinhalese power. The northern kingdom was thus able to initiate a policy of expansion southward. Toward the end of the thirteenth century, its ruler waged a war with the Sinhalese king and gained control over the valuable pearl fishery and some coastal lands. For a brief period the Sinhalese monarch even paid tribute to the northern kingdom. This began a tradition of conflict between the two kingdoms, a conflict which was carried on for a long time with varying results for each side. When the power of the Tamil kingdom was at its height, Ibn Batuta, the famous Arab traveler, visited the capital (1344) and received a friendly welcome from the king. From him we learn that the Tamil king was in control of the coast up to Puttalam and held the pearl fishery. It may also be surmised that the expansion of Islamic power into the far south and the destruction of the Pandyan kingdom in 1334 would have resulted in a movement of Tamil refugees to north Ceylon. This in turn would have strengthened the Tamil kingdom of the north. In the middle of the fourteenth century, the Arya king of the north led an expedition southward and drove the reigning Sinhalese king from his capital at Gampola. As a sequence to this victory, he secured the revenues of some districts in the Sinhalese kingdom. The Tamil kingdom was now at the height of its power, a fact confirmed by both Tamil and Sinhalese tradition.

The rise of a strong leader among the Sinhalese, Alagakonara, to gather its scattered forces and resist the intrusion of the northern army broke the hold that the Tamils had in the Sinhalese areas. Tamil armies had penetrated as far south as Panadura and Gampola but were pushed back after prolonged fighting. The brief revival of Sinhalese power in the fifteenth century under Parakrama Bahu VI once again provoked a direct conflict between the two kingdoms of the north and the south. The Sinhalese armies were led by a brilliant general, an adopted son of the king. His name, Sapumal Kumaraya, is a Sinhalese rendering of the Tamil *Senpaka Perumal*, for he was the son of a Chola nobleman. He invaded the north in 1450, subjugated the Vanni districts, and entered Jaffna. Sinhalese subjects living in Jaffna joined the invaders. The capital fell, and the king escaped to India. Prince Sapumal was made ruler of Jaffna, subject to the overlordship of the king of Kotte. The kingdom of Jaffna was under Sinhalese subjection for about 17 years. Thereafter, the fugitive king, with the help of some south Indian military chiefs, returned to Jaffna, reconquered the kingdom from the Sinhalese viceroy, and re-established the rule of the Arya Chakravartis. The kingdom existed peacefully for the next century and a half. Sinhalese power, after its brief revival, waned once more and was in no position to challenge its northern neighbor. Boundaries were crystallized during this period. The territory between the two kingdoms was by now so jungle-infested and devastated that it was not worth fighting over.

The Tamil kingdom had close relations with the Dravidian power of southern India, the Vijayanagar empire. These emperors, in their expansion southward, sought to bring the island kingdom within their own sphere of influence. In 1385, when Harihara II was emperor, his son led an expedition to the south which crossed over to Ceylon and made the Tamil king a tributary of the empire. We do not know how long this conquest lasted, though we do know that ambassadors of the king were at the Vijayanagar court and that Ceylon is referred to in the inscriptions of the empire as one of its dependencies. Under Deva Raya II, the greatest Vijayanagar emperor, Ceylon was again invaded in 1438. Their suzerainty was probably reimposed on the Tamil kingdom, for it seems to have been accepted thereafter by the Arya Chakravartis. Hence it was that when one of them lost his throne to the Sinhalese, he was able to take refuge in the empire and return with forces supplied by imperial feudatories. When the empire entered a period of decline in the sixteenth century, the protective relationship ceased, and there was no more political contact between the two.

Tamil political organization was modeled on that of the Dravidian states of southern India. The kings adopted the throne names *Pararajasekaran* or *Segarajasekaran*. They used the title *Sethu* in all their official records in memory of their Ramesvaram origins. Their early capital of Singai Nagar was most probably located at Nallur, though, later, with the growth of the port of Jaffna, the kings seem to have shifted to that city. The nucleus of the administration consisted of descendants of thirteenth-century Tamil immigrants. They were of the agricultural caste that performed similar administrative functions in Tamil Nad. These settlers were concentrated in the peninsula near the seat of the capital and royal power. The peninsula was divided into four districts: Valigamam, Vadamarachchi, Thenmarachchi, and Pachchilaipalai. The extensive and fertile lands on the mainland between Mannar and Trincomalee were also divided into districts. The village headman was the official who attended to affairs of the village. Several headmen were supervised by an *adigar*. Heads of each caste group attended to the affairs of that caste and were responsible for the performance of its obligations. Revenue officials called *pandarapillais* went on circuit assessing and collecting revenue.

The northern kingdom was the home of a flourishing trade in the four centuries of its existence. It had the advantage of the Tamil trading tradition in Ceylon and of previously established traders and trading guilds. New ports came into being, and old ones were extended. Jaffna developed into a trading center at this time. The island harbor of Kayts (Urukaturai) became important as a ship-building and repairing center. Mantota was still a major port on the west coast, but the neighboring island of Mannar also came into prominence at this time. On the east coast, Trincomalee continued its historic mercantile role, and Mullaitivu, farther north, also came to be used. The control of the pearl fishery off the coast of Mannar was a great asset to the trade of the kingdom. Pearl divers were imported from Ramesvaram and gradually settled down in and around Mannar. Elephants captured in the Vanni jungles were exported from Jaffna to different parts of northern India. The kings had a substantial navy and were in control of the northern waters. This enabled them to keep up their contacts with southern India, whence they derived support in need. Withdrawal to the mainland after their defeat by the Sinhalese and their return at an opportune moment was made possible by the control of the waters. Their naval strength also enabled them to lead expeditions along the sea into the south of the Sinhalese kingdom. Tamil traders took part in the trade of the Sinhalese ports as well. They were present at Galle in large numbers when this port became an important center of foreign trade in the medieval period. An inscription of the Chinese admiral Cheng Ho in Galle is in three languages—Chinese, Persian, and Tamil. Traders of the Chetty community were settled between Colombo and Negombo.

It was during this period that the Tamils of Ceylon developed a unified social organization and forged some customs of common usage. Up to this time the colonists had been scattered both in time and space and had no opportunity to develop strong institutions. Now, strengthened as they were by a flood of new immigrants and loyalty to a state, the way was open for new outgrowths in social life. This development proceeded up to the modern age and sharply distinguished the Tamils of Ceylon from the Tamils in India, with institutions and social habits different from those of the mother country. It has been generally agreed that many of the immigrants before the eleventh century came from the western part of the Tamil lands, the Malabar coast. The immigrants of the period after that were from the eastern part, the Coromandel coast, driven by the loss of Tamil political power in the motherland. Islamic invasion did away with the Pandyan kingdom, the last independent Tamil state. When Hindu power was re-established with the Vijayanagar empire, it was an expansion of Telugu power southward. The Vijayanagar emperors appointed Telugu lords as tax collectors and military chiefs in the Tamil lands. This especially enraged the propertied and influential Vellalas, who emigrated to what was then the only Tamil kingdom. Immigrants from both Malabar and Coromandel brought aspects of their own social structures, which then merged by the intermingling of these two peoples and produced a set of laws and customs which today prevail among the Ceylon Tamils.

There is today a code of laws called *Thesavalamai* which governs the Tamils of north Ceylon in respect to their rights of property, inheritance, and marriage. It is the codification of custom and usage that existed among the Tamils in the beginning of the eighteenth century, undertaken by a Dutch governor of Ceylon. It is a vital document of the social history of the Ceylon Tamils, for in it are embodied the centuries of development of their customs under the Tamil kingdom of Jaffna. The *Thesavalamai* illustrates the fusion of diverse Tamil customs referred to above. The earlier colonists came from a matriarchal society and brought this feature along with them. In the *Thesavalamai* the property rights of the female are greatly emphasized, thus distinguishing the Ceylon Tamil practice from that of the Tamils of Tamil Nad. Females succeeded females;

the dowry of the mother passed to the daughters. There was a difference between ancestral property and acquired property. The wife had extensive rights over the property that she brought as a dowry and the property that was acquired by her and her husband in married life. The law governing dowry was based on the customs of a matriarchal society. In all these aspects the laws among the Ceylon Tamils were similar to those in vogue among the Malabaris.

This basically matriarchal system was encroached upon by a patriarchal one brought by the flood of colonists from Coromandel. There Brahmanical influences over a long period had created a patriarchal society. The new ideas blended with the old. Thus, in the inheritance of property, the heritage of the father devolved on the son, the dowry on the daughters. Similarly, brothers succeeded to the property of an intestate brother, and sisters to that of a sister. The patriarchal system being a stronger form of social organization, it increasingly asserted itself. Some of the principles of the Hindu joint-family system were assimilated, and these in turn were incorporated into the laws of the people. The position of the father was strengthened. So long as the parents lived, the sons could not claim any of the family property, but had to bring into the common pool everything they earned as bachelors. Property could not be alienated to anyone outside the family without the consent of all the members of the family. These and other principles of Hindu law were superimposed on the Malabar customs then in vogue.

The caste system as it developed among the Tamils of Ceylon shows the basic characteristics of the Dravidian system of south India, with some peculiarities evolved by an immigrant population. As in the case of the Sinhalese, the Brahmanical caste structure had no validity for the Tamils. Indeed, it was even less valid for the Ceylon Tamils than for those of Tamil Nad. The basis of distinction among Dravidian castes seems to have been occupational, with the agricultural castes at the apex of the system. One major difference between the caste system of the Tamils of south India and that of the Tamils of Ceylon was the absence in Ceylon of the important role played by the Brahmin. Especially in the medieval period, there was a great influx of Brahmins into southern India, and these came to occupy the highest caste status. Their role was primarily to act as specialists in ritual, but they were present in such large numbers that they had to perform other functions as well. As the property of their temples was increased, they came to own entire villages and extended their influence over the temporal life of the community as well. Consequently, even under the British they stepped easily into the native bureaucracy and continued their traditional leadership. Among the Ceylon Tamils this development did not take place. In the first place, the Brahmin immigrants were very few; they had not the same pressure to emigrate from the Vijayanagar empire. They were greatly outnumbered by the Vellalas, the leading agriculturalists on whom the Tamil kingdom was based. The Vellalas never gave up their ascendancy and were under no pressure to do so by the Brahmins. The only function of the Brahmins was to perform rituals in temples and at other social ceremonies. Brahmins were, more or less, in the employ of the Vellalas, officiating in temples owned and managed by them. The political and economic ascendancy of the Vellallas has been carried into the modern democratic system by their numerical preponderance.

The Vellalas were thus the key caste in the Tamil social system. They dominated the village and ran its affairs. The numerous other castes served the Vellala. He was a farmer, with centuries of tradition as a tiller of the soil. His position in north Ceylon was comparable with that of his counterpart in Tamil Nad in the early centuries of the Christian era before the influence of Brahmanism had seeped southward.

The Kovias were the caste nearest to the Vellalas in status. They, too, tilled the soil, but they were also obliged to carry the bier to the cremation grounds at Vellala funerals, and they were the barbers and the washermen. The Pallas and Nalavas were landless laborers who worked in the fields of the Vellalas. The Parayas were a caste which had immigrated from India in recent times and settled in segregated spots to perform scavenging considered to be polluting. The last three were the untouchables among the Tamils, with rigorous taboos similar to their counterparts in India. The Nalavas and Kovias were castes peculiar to Ceylon, absent in Tamil Nad. This has led to speculation that they were remnants of Sinhalese settlers in the north enslaved by the Tamils after their conquest and assimilated into their structure.

The fisher castes, divided into a number of groups, stood outside this system and were not associated with the Vellalas in any way. There is evidence to believe that they were the older inhabitants. They occupied the coastal areas all over Ceylon, and some historians feel that the modern Sinhalese fisher caste also originated from these Tamil settlers who were subsequently assimilated. The fisher castes were most numerous in Tamil areas outside Jaffna. They had probably been driven out of Jaffna by the Vellalas once the Vellalas established themselves there. In modern times the fishing castes are still dominant in Mannar, Puttalam, Trincomalee, and Batticaloa. The social ascendancy of the Vellala did not apply in these areas.

In spite of external influences, the caste structure among the Tamils has remained substantially unaltered for centuries, unlike the Sinhalese, among whom recent economic and social changes have altered the whole system. The retention of this old framework of caste has made Tamil society a conservative one, the Jaffna peninsula being more so than the other parts.

From the time of the formation of the Tamil kingdom there was a great concentration of population in the Jaffna peninsula. The average annual rainfall there is from 50 to 75 inches. The country is absolutely flat, and there are no rivers flowing through it. The soil is not exceptionally good. If it was to sustain a large population, it had to be cultivated intensively and made fertile by hard labor. Fortunately, the peninsula has considerable underground water, and this was utilized for lift irrigation. Deep wells were sunk all over the peninsula; the well sweep (*thula*) which levered up the water is still a familiar site on the Jaffna landscape. Paddy was grown in certain parts as a one-season crop. In other parts, vegetable and fruit gardens flourished, and tobacco, which was exported to India. The land was divided into a number of small holdings owned by Vellala families. An average holding was just enough for the sustenance of one family. The basic tax was the grain tax paid in cash. Tax collectors were merely officials of the state, and most taxation was paid directly to the state. Even the lower castes performing the menial tasks had their direct relationship to the state in the form of a poll

tax or a professions tax collected by the head of each caste and paid
to the state. Thus, tenurial rights as well as caste have remained unchanged over a long period.

In the Tamil areas outside the peninsula, paddy was the main crop,
and methods of cultivation were somewhat different from those
adopted in Jaffna. Some of the old irrigation works were still in working order and were used extensively. The Batticaloa and Trincomalee
soil was very fertile and excellent for paddy, and there were a number
of minor irrigation works maintained by communal effort, making possible two crops a year. During the period of general decline in Ceylon's agriculture, these areas were the granary that fed the island's
population. In Batticaloa there were large estates owned by landlords called *podis*. On these estates were settled the tenant-cultivators who tilled the soil and paid rent by working on a portion of
the land set apart for the lord. In the Vanni, a somewhat different
system operated, approximating what is generally termed a feudal
tenure. Here chiefs called Vanniyar exercised authority over wide
tracts of land. Probably the descendants of Tamil warlords hired by
the Sinhalese in the earlier years, they had set themselves up
in these regions when the Sinhalese kingdom receded southward.
Those in the northern half of the dry zone owed their allegiance to
the Jaffna kings, and those in the southern half to the Sinhalese. But
many in the center changed their allegiance as it suited their purposes. The Vanniyar paid to the state an annual fixed tribute. The
way they managed their lands and the tenure of their tenants were
not the concern of the state. The kings did not think it politic to interfere as long as the Vanniyar paid tribute and presented themselves
annually at court as a sign of their allegiance. Sometimes the tribute
took the form of elephants, especially after the elephant trade had
become lucrative. The spirit of sturdy independence nurtured by
such a system lasted a long time among the Vanniyar, who were the
last Tamils to succumb to European domination.

Hinduism in Ceylon has a continuous history from the earliest
Sinhalese colonization of the island. We have seen how Hindu ideas
seeped into Buddhism and how later Hindu and Buddhist coexisted
in many parts of the country. We also saw that there were
many Tamil settlements long before a Tamil kingdom was established

where popular Hindu worship was widely practiced. Under Chola occupation, Hinduism received a great impetus; the magnificent edifices of this period are evidence of their patronage. With the establishment of a Tamil kingdom with a Hindu dynasty, Hinduism was raised to the position of the official religion in a part of the island and thereafter enjoyed all the perquisites of establishment. The Arya dynasty of Jaffna, because of its connection with Ramesvaram, a great center of south Indian Saivism, was deeply conscious of its duties as the patron of Hinduism in Ceylon. The homogeneity of the population, the vast majority being Tamil Hindus, and the patronage of the rulers made Hinduism a vital force in this part of the country. Hinduism became as much a living religion in the north and the east as Buddhism had been in the rest of the island.

The Hindus of Ceylon were, and are, almost exclusively Saivites. Lord Siva was to them the most important god in the Hindu pantheon. Most temples were dedicated to Siva. The *lingam*, symbol of the creative powers of Siva, would be found in wayside shrines. The concept of the Natarajah as the dancing Siva was also very popular among the Tamil Hindus, adorning the temples and the homes of pious Hindus. Second in popularity to Siva was Ganesa, the eldest son of Siva. He was the god of wisdom and was worshipped in educational institutions as well as by the backward peoples living in isolated, less civilized areas. Skanda, also known as Murukan, the second son of Siva, was another well-known deity. The worship of this deity suggests an assimilation of some pre-Aryan cult. The Sinhalese also worshipped Skanda. Among the many other gods and goddesses worshipped in Ceylon, Kannaki is interesting for her place in a legend originating in the Pandyan kingdom and enshrined in the Tamil classic *Silappadikaram*. The goddess Kannaki is held to have come southward to Ceylon and settled in Mullaitivu in northeast Ceylon, where there was a temple dedicated to her. The Sinhalese worshipped her as Pattini. All these deities were introduced from south India, where their worship was a common aspect of Hinduism.

There were some temples and shrines that attracted pilgrims and devotees from all over the island. Perhaps the most important of these was the one at Kataragama, on the banks of the Manik Ganga in south Ceylon. The deity worshipped here was Skanda. Later on it was frequented by Sinhalese as well. The Koneswaram temple at Trincomale was another popular place of worship in medieval times. Yet another was the Tirukethisvaram temple at the port of Mantota. The Munnesvaram temple near Chilaw was another very ancient temple that retained its popularity. The top of Adam's Peak in the central highlands is a place of pilgrimage for both Hindu and Buddhist. Hindus associate this rock with Siva. Within the Jaffna peninsula, the Vallipuram temple on the seacoast near Point Pedro was popular in the middle ages. The underground spring at Keerimalai was held to possess sacred qualities and was a place of pilgrimage. The big Kandaswamy temple in Nallur was the royal temple. Its festivals were elaborate affairs, drawing crowds from all over the peninsula. The ceremonies and festivals were much the same as those in south India, with some slight changes in emphasis. Tamil devotional literature of the Saiva saints was used in worship. Brahmanical influence was less marked than in south India, and it is possible that the Brahmins of Ceylon were not as well versed in Sanskrit as those of India. The Hindu New Year falling in the middle of April was more elaborately celebrated than among the Tamils of India, while festivities of a northern origin such as Deepavali and Navarathri were not observed as colorfully as in India. Among the more backward peoples and lower castes demonology was practiced. In the remoter villages there were roadside shrines to demons (*munis*), who were propitiated by token offerings.

The contribution of the Tamils to the art of Ceylon is part of the major stream of Dravidian influence over the centuries. In our review of Sinhalese art we saw how periodic waves of Dravidian influence affected the architecture and sculpture of the Sinhalese. But the great age of the art of Ceylon, both Sinhalese and Tamil, seems to have ended with the thirteenth century. The period of decline affected both these cultural groups equally. The Tamil kingdom did not indulge in any great architectural activity because it did not have the resources to do so. Constant fighting swallowed up considerable revenue. The temples built by the Tamils were of medium size and in the Madura style of the Vijayanagar period. A feature of this style was the ornate and heavily sculptured *gopuram*, or tower, at the entrance. The temples of Jaffna all followed this style. None of the large temples remains today, due partly to the hostility of the Portuguese. No original artistic tradition grew in Tamil Ceylon. Culturally, the Tamils looked upon their arts as part of the Dravidian tradition of south India. When any major work was to be undertaken, craftsmen would be brought from Tamil Nad. Geographic proximity and close political relations made this possible. An expert artist of Jaffna would soon cross the straits to gain wider recognition in India.

In the literary and educational sphere, the Ceylon Tamils developed stronger traditions and made significant contributions. The kings were great patrons of literature, and some of them were poets and writers of merit. From an early date, education spread among the people, creating a literate community which remains so to this day. Temple schools and improvised classes on the outer verandah of the village schoolmaster's house spread basic education to the rural areas. Toward the end of the fifteenth century, an academy of Tamil literature was founded at Nallur by the king. This academy did useful work in collecting and preserving ancient classical Tamil works in manuscript form. Some historical literature was attempted in this period and some translations and adaptations from Sanskrit works. Medicine and astrology were two subjects whose study attained high standards in Jaffna. Some original medical treatises were written at this time. A school of Ayurveda called Siddha was preserved in Jaffna up to modern times. Astrology was studied and practiced widely. The calculation of good and bad days according to planetary position was done by experts. Casting of horoscopes at birth and the comparison of horoscopes before marriage were popular. In certain families, *expertise* in his art has been handed down to the present day. Tamil was also nurtured in the later Sinhalese kingdoms, and some works were composed in Tamil. The Tamil spoken and written in Ceylon is freer of Sanskrit influence than that in south India. Some archaic forms that are lost on the mainland have been retained in Jaffna.

By the sixteenth century, the Tamils were established as a people in the island. They had a well-defined territorial area which they had carved out as their permanent home. They had ceased looking to their original homeland except for cultural inspiration. They were a political entity with sovereignty, which they preserved from Sinhalese encroachment. They were developing social institutions and eco-

nomic attitudes to suit their new environment. These new developments separated them from the Tamils of India, a separation that,
under the colonial powers, was to become more marked. Their distinctiveness from the Sinhalese, the other major community in the
island, was also great. They spoke a totally different language; they
professed a different religion. Occupying two different parts of the
country with widely different geographical and physical environ-
ments, the two communities developed distinct economic patterns
and attitudes toward life. There was, further, the heritage of political
animosity and frequent conflict. But, inhabiting a small island, the
history of these two peoples had necessarily to converge. In the course
of the sixteenth century, they were both exposed in a similar manner
to the arrival of Europeans. This was bound to bring them together
and create as many problems as when they had been independent
entities.

FOUR

THE MUSLIMS OF CEYLON

The Muslims of Ceylon, now totaling six and a half per cent of the entire population, are divided into various groups. The bulk of them call themselves Ceylon Moors, after the name given to them by the Portuguese who first landed on the island. Their earliest origins are somewhat obscure. It is a well-established fact that there was a brisk commerce between South Asia and the West from pre-Christian times. Because of the obvious advantage of their geographical location, the inhabitants of the Arabian peninsula have been the traditional carriers of this trade. But for a long time the Arabs did not come to Ceylon, because the produce of this island could be collected from the great emporia of the Malabar coast. Only later did there develop a desire to establish direct contacts with Ceylon and secure its products first-hand. In the earliest phase of this direct trade with Ceylon, Persians appeared as the traders. There is evidence of a seventh-century Persian Christian colony settled for purposes of trade in Ceylon. With the spread of Islam and the Arab language in the Middle East at this time, these peoples acquired a new unity and idealism which gave fresh impetus to their commercial activity. Now they appeared in the Eastern waters under the name Arabs and, from the ninth century onward, began to dominate the trade from the Far East to Africa. We hear of the establishment of Arab trading colonies in almost all major trading stations of the East along the great East-West highway, including Ceylon.

Ceylon, known to the Arabs as Serendib, was the home of precious stones, pearls, and ivory. Cinnamon later became an important attraction. The earliest Arab colonies, of about the tenth century, seem to have been established by agents of the principal traders of the south Indian ports to supply them with the goods of Ceylon. The gems of Ceylon were greatly valued in the Middle East, and one of the early Arab names of the island meant "Island of the Gems." An early tradition records that in the eighth century some widows and orphans of Arab colonists in Ceylon were repatriated by the Sinhalese king. In the Muslim cemetery at Colombo a Cufic inscription of the tenth century has been discovered. At about the same time, Islam appeared in Malabar as a missionary force, and the account records the visit of these Muslim fakirs to Ceylon. The mountain known as Adam's Peak, sacred to Hindus and Buddhists, now became a place of pilgrimage for Muslims as the abode of Adam, their primitive father. These pilgrimages were evidently utilized for trade operations as well, to make contact with the interior, especially with the reputed gem country which was on the road. The Sinhalese kings realized the value of this increasing Arab interest in the island and encouraged more and more Arab settlements. One feature which eased their path greatly was the tolerance shown by the Sinhalese in matters of religion. A number of settlements arose on the western coast at points suitable for the berthing of ships.

From the eleventh century onward there was a tremendous increase in Arab shipping and commerce in the Indian Ocean. The southern tip of India, known to the Arabs as Ma'bar, became their special focus of trade. Far Eastern, South Asian, and Western goods changed hands here in ever-increasing quantities. Success in trade went hand in hand with success in proselytization. In Malabar and in the southern tip of the Indian peninsula there came into existence Islamic concentrations of Arabs and converted Indians. Their economic and religious homogeneity cut them off from the rest of the population and enabled them to develop as a powerful force where they were established. They had their own leaders who had influential connection with the Arab trading complex and were extremely wealthy. They could provide what the ruler wanted and fetch the best prices for his produce. The ruler, therefore, did not seek to extend over them the arm of the state's authority. The Muslim community thus looked after itself, followed its own customs and its own laws. It was this system that was reproduced in Ceylon, though in less intensive form. In Ceylon the southern ports were controlled by these Arab communities under a head who was recognized as a delegate of the sovereign. They collected customs dues and supervised shipping. They advised the king on matters of trade. The embassy of Bhuvaneka Bahu I to the Egyptian court in 1283, with a view to establishing direct trade relations with that kingdom, was planned and executed by the king's Arab advisers.

In the fourteenth century, when the Sinhalese kings were being pressed by the expanding Tamil kingdom and its maritime influence, they came to rely more heavily on the southern Muslim community. When Colombo and Negombo were attacked by the Tamils, the Arabs organized the defense. The Tamils of the north and the Arabs were competitors, for the Tamil traders of the northern kingdom did considerable sailing of their own to the Indian coast and as far as Yemen. The decline of Tamil power in the fifteenth century left the trade of the south completely in Muslim hands. Their ports of Colombo and Galle grew in importance, and they extended their settlements to other ports along the coast. The nature of their trade also expanded. It was no longer limited to the few luxury goods that Ceylon produced. Pepper and cinnamon that grew wild were exported in large quantities. Areca nuts were taken to the Indian markets. Muslims now began to participate in the brisk trade between India and Ceylon. Their influence also spread to the interior. They took to peddling goods from ports to the hinterland and from the villages back to port. Their role now touched the community at vital spots. Some interior village settlements of Muslims came into existence. Village headmen were appointed from their numbers, and they became landowners as well.

It is interesting to examine how this numerical increase came about, who the new people were, and where they came from. They were certainly not all of them Arabs. In the early stages when there were small colonies of Arab traders, the population, for obvious reasons, would have been predominantly male. These Arabs married the people with whom they came into contact, both Sinhalese and

Tamils. Conversion of the Indians to Islam increased the number of such intermarriages. The Arab communities of Ceylon naturally looked for strength to their coreligionists across the straits and established closer relations with them. Their numbers were augmented by immigration of Indian Muslims from the opposite coast, and together they carried on the Indo-Ceylon trade and the coastal trade of Ceylon. The places where they settled were well suited for their purpose. Besides the early Arab settlements on the southwestern coast, Muslim towns and villages rose in Chilaw, Puttalam, Mannar, Jaffna town, Trincomalee, and Batticaloa. After the decline of the caliphate of Baghdad in the second half of the thirteenth century, Arab activities in the Indian Ocean were not on the same scale as before. The Muslim community of Ceylon began to look to India for its cultural inspiration, for by this time Muslims held a dominant position on the west coast of India. Thus, by the fifteenth century the Muslim settlements of Ceylon had lost their exclusively Arab character and had become Indo-Arab.

This dual origin of the Ceylonese Muslims is enshrined in traditions persisting among them concerning their past history. One tradition has it that the earliest settlers came from Arabia in the early part of the eighth century as part of a wave of fugitives from oppressive rule. These fugitives colonized southern India, Ceylon, and Malacca. Whatever the truth in this tradition, it does reflect the Arabian origins of a part of the Ceylonese Muslim community. Another tradition refers to the colonization of certain villages by Muslim settlers from Kayalpatnam, a town on the Madura coast, one of the earliest Muslim strongholds and a center of Islamic culture. A very close connection exists between Muslim settlements in the north and east of the island and those in south India. The origin of these island people from the coastal Muslim communities of Tamil Nad is undoubted. Even in the veins of the Arab descendants of the south Ceylon settlements, there must have been mixed the blood of the Muslims of the opposite coast. In any case, such mixing would have been inevitable after the sixteenth century, when Portuguese conquest put an end to any influx from Arabia.

After the sixteenth century, the Muslim community of Ceylon became completely "Ceylonized." One of the first spheres of that

"Ceylonization" was in language. The greatest influence on the Muslims was the Tamil language, for it was the Tamil community they confronted most in the Indo-Ceylon trading operations. Tamil was an important language of South Asian commerce. And Islam had achieved some success in the conversion of a few of the coastal Tamil communities. Over the years Tamil became the mother tongue of a great majority of the Muslims of Ceylon. That language, because of contact with Arabic, changed somewhat at the hands of its Muslim speakers. Arabic words were adopted, especially in religious terminology. In written Tamil some new letters were improvised to represent Arabic sounds absent in the Tamil alphabet. Later this fusion came to be known as Arabic-Tamil, in which a considerable body of Islamic literature flourished. Those Muslims who were native Tamil converts continued to use their own language, speaking and writing with the same fluency and facility as the Tamils themselves possessed. Sections of the Muslim community in the north and east of the island used the language with perfect ease and produced writers and poets of merit. Those Muslims settled in Sinhalese areas learned to speak Sinhalese very fluently; nevertheless their home language, in a great many cases, continued to be Tamil.

Some of the Tamil customs were also absorbed by the Muslims. Many of these pertained to marriage; understandably, because of the extensive practice of intermarriage that took place with Tamil converts. The parents' gift of a dowry (*stridhanam*) to the bride was a Tamil custom prevalent among the Ceylon Muslims. In the marriage ceremony many of the aspects of a Hindu marriage were taken over. Bedecking the bridegroom with jewels and the *alatti* ceremony of blessing the couple with a tray of burning wicks were practiced by the Muslims. Further, the bridegroom tied a nuptial knot (*thali*) around the bride's neck as a symbol of union. Purdah was less rigorously practiced and the women were comparatively freer than in orthodox societies.

In the sixteenth century, when the Portuguese were struggling to implant their power in maritime Ceylon, the Muslims were deeply affected by these events. The Portuguese came to the East as sworn enemies of Islam, and their early activities in these waters showed the extent of their indiscriminate hostility to anyone professing this faith. The more crucial factor in this hostility was, of course, economic, as it was the Muslims who dominated Asian trade which the Portuguese wanted to capture by the oceanic route. In the narrower context of Ceylon, when the local kingdoms were struggling to preserve their independence, they found the Muslims firm allies against a common foe. The external contacts of the local Muslims were valuable avenues to securing foreign help, and Muslims fought in Sinhalese armies with great courage. Though none of these efforts was of any avail against the superior navies of the Portuguese, they endeared the Muslims to the Sinhalese and strengthened the community of interests between them. At this time the Muslims secured a greater stake in the country; they were given gifts of land for their services and became landed proprietors. Also at this time, some dispersal of Muslims took place into Sinhalese villages as Portuguese power expanded in the coastal areas.

The biggest migration that took the Muslims into the central highlands occurred in the beginning of the seventeenth century. By this time the Portuguese were masters of the entire seacoast of the southwest and issued orders expelling Muslims from these territories. The Sinhalese king of Kandy offered the Muslims asylum, and they moved in large numbers into the interior. He settled them in villages near Kandy. They soon extended their peddling trade all over the kingdom and helped the king to develop his trade through those ports that were still left in his hands. Many of the Muslims chose to settle on the east coast of the island, an area that was under the kings of Kandy. Here they settled in a long belt from Batticaloa southward for about 60 miles. Many of them became farmers and established a rural tradition. The largest rural settlements of Muslims today are in this belt. They form a majority of the population of the area and have been able, in modern times, to send several elected representatives of their faith to the Ceylon Parliament.

In the eighteenth century, the Muslim community had a further increase in numerical strength with the immigration of Malays from the Archipelago. This immigration was carried out under the auspices of the Dutch, who, at this time, controlled Ceylon and the East Indian Islands. They found it profitable to transport Malay regiments to defend their positions in Ceylon. Other Malays were exiled to Ceylon for political reasons. In Ceylon they had a reputation as good soldiers. When the British replaced the Dutch, these Malays joined the British regiments. They spoke the Malay language among themselves, thus preserving their individuality from the other Muslims.

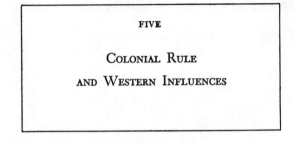

FIVE

COLONIAL RULE
AND WESTERN INFLUENCES

PORTUGUESE RULE IN CEYLON AND ITS LEGACY

In the beginning of the sixteenth century there were three centers of political power in Ceylon—Kotte, Kandy, and Jaffna. Kotte, the strongest kingdom, controlled all the lands to the south and southwest, including the cinnamon woods and the western ports. It was the chief seat of Sinhalese power, a skeletal relic of the great kingdoms of the classical age. The kings of Kotte claimed overlordship over Kandy and, indeed, over the whole island, the latter claim being even more imaginary than the former. Toward the end of the fifteenth century, some military lords set themselves up in the strategic safety of the central highlands. With the city of Kandy as their capital, they established an independent political power that had nothing much other than natural barriers to uphold it. Jaffna was the seat of Tamil power, with an existence independent of the two Sinhalese kingdoms. In terms of actual political power and economic means, rapid decline and utter weakness characterized the whole scene at this period. None of the kingdoms had the potential to emerge as the leader of a reunification of the island or even to assert itself decisively over the other two. Culturally and linguistically the country was divided in two, and there was little contact between the separate parts. Indeed, the island may be said to have been divided into three kingdoms and two nations. It was in this condition that the island was exposed to the first wave of Western influence.

A mixture of motives—political and economic, geographic and religious—had driven the tiny Iberian nation of Portugal to undertake a series of steps that eventually ended in one of the most momentous events in maritime history, from which in turn flowed a series of historic consequences. This was the discovery of the oceanic route from Europe to India around the Cape of Good Hope. The great movement thus inaugurated left its impact on several countries and brought an economically progressive West face to face with a technically stagnant or even declining East. The coming of the Portuguese into the Eastern waters ushered in what has been aptly termed the Vasco da Gama Epoch in Asian history. Though Ceylon's first contact with the Portuguese was somewhat fortuitous—it was caused by adverse winds which drove Lourenco de Almeida's fleet into Colombo in 1505—it was obvious that sooner or later the Portuguese, in their attempt to dominate the Indian Ocean, must set foot on Ceylon. Don Lourenco, son of the Portuguese viceroy of India, was cruising in the Indian Ocean from the new Portuguese fort at Cochin when he was blown into Colombo. He was promptly taken to the king of Kotte, with whom he had a friendly audience. When the Portuguese left Colombo for Cochin, they took with them some cinnamon and two elephants, together with an impression of the commercial possibilities of the island.

An agreement was subsequently entered into with the king of Kotte by which the king promised the Portuguese a regular supply of cinnamon and permitted them to establish a residence in Colombo for purposes of trade. Very soon it became obvious that the newly arrived traders differed from the several other nationalities who frequented the ports of Ceylon in both their aims and their methods. They were exceptionally well armed, and tales of their activities in the Indian waters showed their monopolistic intentions. They were particularly hostile to Muslim traders, whose vessels they attacked and plundered on sight. In Ceylon they very soon requested the king's permission to build a fort to protect their trade in Colombo. They also asked him to expell all Muslim traders from his ports. The king very reluctantly acceded to the former, but he rejected the latter as impracticable. The fort was built in 1518 but was soon abandoned because of popular hostility. The Portuguese had by this time a good idea of the strategic importance of settlements in Ceylon to protect their coastal establishments in India and to further their over-all aims of dominating the trade of the Indian Ocean. They had also tasted sufficiently of the profits of Ceylon's trade to create an appetite for more. But of territorial ambitions they had as yet none in Ceylon.

At this stage the kingdom of Kotte, the strongest power in the island, suffered a series of events which signified its political disintegration. A palace revolution was enacted against the reigning king in 1521 by three of his sons, and the kingdom was partitioned among them. The eldest brother, Bhuvaneka Bahu, ruled at Kotte, and the two others set up centers of independent authority in Sitawake and Rayigama. The further fragmentation of a kingdom which was only one of three divisions in a small island was a damaging blow to an already shaky structure. The brother ruling at Rayigama died shortly after, leaving the other two inveterate rivals for the lands along the southwestern border. Under these circumstances, to call in Portuguese assistance was a temptation the ruler of Kotte could not resist. The Portuguese were thereby drawn into the island's politics, an opportunity they were not reluctant to exploit. Mayadunne, the rival ruler at Sitawake, was much the abler ruler, and his expansionist policy drove his brother at Kotte to greater dependence on the Portuguese. The Portuguese rescued the king from many a difficult situation when he was closely besieged by Mayadunne, who had the support of the navy of the Zamorin of Calicut, the most powerful ruler of the Malabar coast. A common hostility to the Portuguese had brought these two South Asian rulers together. The superior strength of the Portuguese always triumphed in the end, and Bhuvaneka Bahu was filled with gratitude for his Western protectors.

Bhuvaneka Bahu became a Portuguese protégé, dependent on Portuguese arms for his very existence. As he grew old, he began to think of the succession to his throne. To ensure the smooth succession of his direct descendant, his grandson Dharmapala, he decided to secure Portuguese recognition and support for his heir. An image of the prince was sent to Lisbon, where the king of Portugal crowned it king of Ceylon with great pomp in 1543 and guaranteed to protect the king on the throne and defend his kingdom against all attack. In return, the Portuguese were confirmed in all their privileges and were promised the continuous payment of a tribute in cinnamon. The fort at Colombo was rebuilt on a grander scale and made defensible with ramparts and bastions. The aging king of Kotte died in 1551, but, as Prince Dharmapala was yet a minor, his father was appointed regent. The prince was entrusted to the Franciscans to be educated. So successful were they that in 1557 his conversion to Christianity was effected. This was a great milestone in the expansion of Portuguese power in Ceylon.

The young king of Kotte, with his conversion to Christianity, became far more dependent on the Portuguese than his predecessor had ever been. To the great majority of his people this act of conversion had disqualified him from the throne. For the one continuous factor in Sinhalese history had been the connection between Buddhism and the state. The rival king of Sitawake, already at war with Kotte, was the principal beneficiary of this development. He succeeded in attracting the loyalty of the people by holding up the king of Kotte as a puppet of a foreign power. Now this line of propaganda could be made even more deadly and its effects even more disastrous to the Kotte dynasty. Very soon the king of Sitawake had annexed large parts of the original Kotte kingdom and was pressing on the capital city itself. The Portuguese now found that their greatly increased status and prestige brought with it a disproportionate share of responsibilities and commitments. As the king of Sitawake had chosen an anti-Portuguese front to attack his rival, the Portuguese were morally and materially obliged to defend King Dharmapala. To such an extent was Dharmapala devoid of all control of the kingdom that the Portuguese themselves had to fight the war as their own and bear the brunt of Mayadunne's attack. They thus took control of whatever was left of the Kotte administration. When the war in the interior was going heavily against Dharmapala, they decided to abandon Kotte and retreated to Colombo, taking the king with them. Dharmapala was now not even a puppet king; he became a member of the Portuguese entourage, a part of the assets and liabilities of the Portuguese on the island.

The withdrawal from Kotte to Colombo was the end of the Kotte kingdom and left the field free to Mayadunne of Sitawake. Portuguese power was confined, as was also the authority of Dharmapala, to the city of Colombo. In 1581 Mayadunne was succeeded by his even more intrepid son Rajasinha, who continued to fight. More than once he laid siege to Colombo, and it was only the timely arrival of reinforcements from Goa that saved the situation. The Portuguese control of the seas enabled them to keep this toe hold on the island when everything within the country had gone against them. And the absence of sea power was the only obstacle to prevent the Sinhalese from getting rid of the foreigner. Rajasinha of Sitawake could not maintain pressure on Colombo for long. The fall of Sitawake was as rapid as its rise. In 1593 Rajasinha died, and the kingdom disintegrated for want of a strong successor. The Portuguese regained their position within the country and recaptured all the lands that the Kotte kingdom had lost. Sitawake was no more, and Kotte now achieved the fullest territorial extent it had held before partition. While these events were taking place, Dharmapala was in the position of an interested spectator, being unable to change the course of events one way or another. In 1580, on the advice of the Franciscans, he made out a deed donating his dominions after his death to King Henry of Portugal. The gift was accepted on behalf of the king by the Portuguese captain-general. After an increasingly miserable old age, Dharmapala died in 1597. The captain-general took formal possession of the kingdom, and thereafter the Portuguese were sovereigns of a large part of the country.

As these events were taking place in the south, a similar set of circumstances was entangling the Portuguese in the affairs of the Jaffna kingdom in the north. The missionaries were the first to enter this kingdom. Following on his phenomenal proselytizing success on the fishery coast off Tuticorin in the southern tip of India, St. Francis Xavier sent one of his disciples of the same name to Mannar, inhabited by people closely related to those in Tuticorin. He, too, was remarkably successful, and by the end of 1544 almost the entire island of Mannar had been converted to Catholicism. The reaction of Sangily, king of Jaffna, was prompt and severe. He led an expedition to Mannar and decapitated almost all the converts, about six hundred in all, and their priest. This was treated by the king of Portugal as a great affront and had to be avenged if the process of conversion was to make any further headway. The moment was not then opportune for the Portuguese to send an expedition, and after their heavy involvements in Kotte they could not distract their attention from their major task on the island. Very soon, however, internal rivalries in Jaffna played into Portuguese hands, and the king's brother, a contestant to the throne, sought Portuguese assistance. King Sangily further antagonized the Portuguese by giving asylum to Sinhalese leaders who were fighting the Portuguese. Finally, in 1560 the expedition to Jaffna was fitted out under Viceroy Braganza.

The Portuguese army was initially very successful. In spite of determined resistance by the Tamils, the superior artillery of the Portuguese had great effect. The capital was taken, and the king fled with the bulk of his treasures. The Portuguese pursued him, but he escaped to the Vanni (mainland). Mounting popular opposition made it difficult for the Portuguese to hold their positions and keep open the communication line to their ships. They decided to withdraw and leave the peninsula, their mission to subjugate the king unaccomplished. It was a great humiliation to the viceroy, who, to save face, decided to capture the island of Mannar. This was completed in 1561, and a fort was built for the defense of the garrison. Christians from the fishery coast of Ceylon were settled on Mannar, giving the Portuguese a commanding position over the pearl fishery there. Later kings of Jaffna made several attempts to recapture Mannar, but none was successful.

The second Portuguese invasion (1591) was more successful than the first. A hostile king at Jaffna was proving to be a nuisance. He was aiding the king of Kandy, against whom the Portuguese were now at war. His attitude was an obstacle to the extension of missionary activity among the Tamils; the priests were clamoring for the conquest of Jaffna. In this second attack, the Tamils were utterly routed and the king captured and slain. Not wishing to undertake the administration of Jaffna directly, the Portuguese raised one of the Tamil princes to the throne as a vassal of the Portuguese with the obligation of paying an annual tribute. A Portuguese garrison was stationed in Jaffna for the protection of the king and the maintenance of Portuguese interests. When this king died, there was further trouble in Jaffna. Succession was disputed and the anti-Portuguese popular

sentiment was crying out for a leader. Sangily Kumara, who succeeded in establishing himself as king, tried to shake off his dependence on the Portuguese. He had dealings with the Nayak of Tanjore
and even attempted relations with the Dutch, who had already
come on the scene. The captain-general sent an expedition to settle
scores with the king. The king was seized and deported to Goa, and
in 1619 the kingdom annexed by the Portuguese.

Now the Portuguese were in direct possession of the entire island
except for the central highlands and the eastern coast. These parts
belonged to the kingdom centered at Kandy, which, as the last remnant of Sinhalese political power, now began to play an increasingly
important role in the island's history. It emerged in its new role as
custodian of Sinhalese nationalism under an able nobleman from
Kandy who set himself up on the throne in the teeth of Portuguese
opposition. The Portuguese sought to repeat their success in Kotte
and set up a protégé queen on the throne, baptized as a Christian
and supported with Portuguese arms. This ended in a disastrous Portuguese defeat in 1594, when the Kandyans were led by this nobleman, who became king as Wimala Dharma Surya. The new kingdom
was thus founded on an anti-Portuguese platform, and the Portuguese spent the half century making futile attempts to reduce this
kingdom. Succeeding commanders extended Portuguese authority
into the interior and brought the country under their administrative
control up to the hills. They took control of the two east coast ports,
Trincomalee and Batticaloa, and gained mastery of the island's trade.
But they were not able to proceed farther and conquer Kandy. Pun-
itive raids into the hill country were only temporarily successful, and
no sooner did the army withdraw than the Kandyan king resumed
control. In one of these expeditions in 1630, the whole army, including the captain-general, was trapped and massacred by the Kandyans.
This was the second major disaster in the history of Portuguese activities in Ceylon. Besides maintaining their own independence, the
Kandyans were soon able to exercise their influence in the Portu-
guese-administered lowlands. As the only remaining Sinhalese kingdom, they gained more and more prestige and took over leadership of
nationalist elements in the lowlands. Thus they fomented and supported rebellion, accepted refugees, and were a great obstacle to the

pacification by the Portuguese of newly acquired lands. And it was Kandyan strategy that brought the Dutch to the island and led eventually to the expulsion of the Portuguese.

For about half a century (1597-1656), the Portuguese directly administered a belt of territory from Chilaw to the Walawa Ganga, including the most heavily populated districts of the island. The Portuguese government of Ceylon was part of what they grandiloquently termed *Estado da India*, indeed an important part of their Eastern possessions. This Eastern empire was ruled from Goa, where the viceroy, as representative of the king, maintained his seat of government. Subordinate to the viceroy, the captain-general was the head of the government in Ceylon. Because of the distance, the size of the territories, and the nature of the problems involved, he had a wide measure of discretion and power. Within the country the captain-general soon stepped into the shoes of the king of Kotte. He had a grand establishment at Malwana, about ten miles east of Colombo. He affected all the external symbols of sovereignty that were practiced traditionally by Sinhalese royalty. In the eyes of the Sinhalese he was the king who had come to replace their traditional monarchs.

The Portuguese inherited a long-standing native administrative structure that was closely tied up with the nature of landholding. Officials performed functions for which they were remunerated in land. However much the Portuguese may have desired to run the country in their own way, the odds were heavily on the side of continuing undisturbed the traditional structure, with changes at the top to signify the change of masters. Hence the old offices and administrative divisions continued into the new era. The old kingdom had been divided into four provinces with *Dissavas* in charge, and provinces were subdivided into *korales*, *pattus*, and villages. The *Dissava* was an important officer with revenue, military, and judicial powers in the province. The Portuguese gradually replaced the Sinhalese in this office with their own men. Some top Sinhalese chiefs whose loyalty was suspect or whose influence was potentially dangerous were banished to Goa or even to Portugal. The lower territorial offices were retained in their existing form and with existing personnel insofar as the latter were not disloyal. Cutting across this territorial system was a departmental one, involving a few occupations performed by separate castes. The most important of these as far as the Portuguese were concerned were the departments responsible for the production of cinnamon and for the capture and supply of elephants. Each of these had a head, or *Vidana,* whose duty it was to procure supplies for the state and mobilize labor for this purpose. This native machinery could be used for achieving the aims of Portuguese policy. The policy toward the native military system was much the same. Under the existing system, military service to the state was an obligation due for holding a plot of land. The forces thus collected were known as the *lascarins,* organized under their own officials. The Portuguese now took over these forces and used them extensively in their wars in the island. There seems to have been no formal promise to continue the existing customs and institutions, and the later belief in a Convention of Malwana at which such a promise was made seems to have been a misguided impression of later times. But the policies followed by the Portuguese showed their intention to cause no radical break in the social organization of the country, and it was this which gave rise to the idea of a Convention of Malwana as a guarantee of native rights and customs.

However reluctant the Portuguese may have been to bring about radical changes, the very fact that a foreign hand was at the helm of affairs resulted in many innovations. Some of these arose from the manner in which the old system was run. The new rulers' ignorance of the details of the administrative structure and their understandable reluctance to interfere too much led to a great expansion of the power of the Sinhalese chiefs at the expense of the service tenants. Their judicial and administrative powers over the people increased, and many of them became rich in this period through abuse of service obligations. To this oppression was added that of the Portuguese themselves, who filled the higher administrative appointments. The results of this relaxation of direct central control and of the arbitrary behavior of Portuguese *fidalgos* and Sinhalese nobles were reflected in complaints made by the common people that reached the ears of the king of Portugal.

An innovation made by the Portuguese was to set up a separate and independent branch of government to manage revenue affairs. No such division was known under the traditional system. It was a change in keeping with methods used in the home country. The superintendent of revenue was a powerful officer, in control of all avenues that produced revenue to the central government. This officer was quite independent of the captain-general, and often there were clashes over their undefined boundaries of power.

Considerable innovations were made in the system of landholding and the relations between state and landholder. Under the Kotte kingdom, a graded system of service and obligations had culminated in the person of the king, who, as in all Indian theory, owned the land. It admitted of no change and appealed to custom and usage as its sanction. Its main *raison d'être* was the requirement that a king, with little or no surplus income, maintain the administration of a large kingdom. The Portuguese used gifts of land to gain political support and made lavish grants of villages to *fidalgos* and converted Sinhalese chiefs. The recipient enjoyed all taxes and obligatory serv-ices from the tenants in the village and gave a fixed sum to the state as quitrent. It was sought in this way to encourage a Portuguese set-tler colony on which Portuguese power could be firmly based. The settlers were to be a landowning aristocracy, through whom the re-sources of the country could be developed. The policy did not work out in this way. Not many *fidalgos* were prepared to settle down to the arduous and isolated life of a farmer, nor did they have the tradi-tions of an agricultural class. The new owners were thus, for the most part, absentee landlords living in the towns and farming out the rev-enues of their villages to Sinhalese collectors for a fixed remittance. The status of the ordinary farmer remained unchanged throughout this period. Consequently, these innovations left no lasting effects on the social organization of the Sinhalese. Nor did they lead to any improvements in agricultural techniques.

The land policy did, however, increase exactions from the peas-ants. The type of service now demanded by the state was more severe than earlier. Because of the pressing need for soldiers throughout a greater part of Portuguese rule, many of the tenants were forced into military service in place of their other, less difficult obligations. With a view to encouraging trade in the products of Ceylon, landholders were called upon to pay part of their quitrent in produce such as pep-per and areca nuts. This caused great hardship, as the quantity required was very high, and the peasant had sometimes to purchase these articles to pay his tax. These factors were responsible for the undercurrent of hostility toward Portuguese land policy.

One of the great enterprises of the Portuguese was to compile a *tombo*, or land register. The purpose of this difficult undertaking was to get a definite picture of the revenues that could be derived from every holding in the Kotte kingdom. The Portuguese authorities in Goa and in Portugal had, before their conquest of Ceylon, been led to think of the island as a potential El Dorado, and this had encouraged them to suffer the expenditure and troubles of outright conquest. The first years of sovereign administration produced heavy deficits, and the Crown suspected that much of the revenue was filling private pockets. In addition, a large amount of land had been taken from the Buddhist temples and given by Dharmapala to the various Catholic orders working in Ceylon. An accurate land register could eradicate these evils. In each register the boundaries of villages and *korales* and of individual landholdings in each village would be entered. There were to be parallel entries of the customary obligations of each cultivator. The superintendent of revenue and his secretary visited each *korale*, summoned all the inhabitants to a central spot, inspected their claims and titles, and then entered these in the book. Grants to individuals or religious institutions were entered in a separate book, though the religious orders that enjoyed such grants did not generally cooperate in this venture. Similar registers were later compiled for the Jaffna area as well. Some of these are extant in the Lisbon archives, invaluable evidence for a study of land tenure of the seventeenth century.

One of the most lasting influences of Portuguese rule in Ceylon was that exerted through their religious policy. A cursory glance at Portuguese activities overseas shows the extent to which religion influenced their actions and policies. "Spices and Christians" were what they had come to the East for; in some cases they started looking for Christians even before they could get at the spices. In Ceylon the first missionaries were active long before the Portuguese acquired political power. Taking advantage of the tolerance of the Sinhalese king and his friendship toward the Portuguese, Franciscans arrived in 1543 and started to proselytize among the coastal communities. In these early days, success in the north was greater than among the Sinhalese. It was with the conversion of Dharmapala that the missionary movement took great strides forward among the upper classes. Toward the end of the sixteenth century, the monopoly of the Franciscans was broken, and Jesuits, Dominicans, and Augustinians appeared, in spite of attempts by the Franciscans to block the entry of other orders. Extensive lands belonging to Buddhist and Hindu temples were confiscated and given to the Catholic orders, which thus became very affluent, exciting the jealousy of the king of Portugal himself.

The first ecclesiastical council held at Goa in 1567 had laid down broad principles on which to operate missionary work in India. Forced conversion was repudiated, but the worship of other religions was not to be permitted within Portuguese territory. In Ceylon, the extensive powers of patronage and preference in appointments could be used to make Christianity attractive. Only Christians were appointed to the important offices, and the nobility, rather than lose their traditional positions of leadership, preferred to shed their traditional faith. Many of the landed aristocracy became Christians and took Portuguese names at baptism. Old Sinhalese families took on surnames such as Fernando, de Silva, Pieris, de Andrado, de Costa, and are still known by these names. There was also considerable success among the Tamils of north Ceylon, where several churches were constructed in the villages. Conversion was particularly effective among the fishing communities, both Sinhalese and Tamil. In both India and Ceylon these communities seem to have been very receptive to Christian preaching, and it was among them that it became a mass religion. Very many explanations, economic, sociological, and mystic, have been given for this interesting phenomenon, some of which are plausible, others fantastic. To this day the descendants of many of these sixteenth-century converts have remained faithful to their religion.

How far these conversions were forced is a question fraught with emotion in modern Ceylon. Under the influence of a Buddhist revival, it is a popular view that Catholicism was introduced by the Portuguese at the point of the sword. Probably none of the conversions were forced, on a strict interpretation of the term *force*. But a

great deal of indirect compulsion was brought to bear by the prohibi-
tion of the public practice of Buddhism and Hinduism and the impoverishment and even destrùction of their institutions. Some famous Buddhist and Hindu temples were destroyed and churches
constructed in their very precincts. Both these religions lacked an
independent organization and were dependent on state support for
their survival. The Buddhist *bhikkhus* fled into the kingdom of
Kandy, where they were well received. Buddhism ceased to exist in
the low country as a popular religion. The void created by the denial
of the old customs of worship and of the spiritual nourishment they
had provided was filled by Christianity, and this in part explains the
success of the conversions. Christianity was presented in a form that
could be comprehended by and acceptable to the common people.
The process of adaptation boldly and successfully carried out by some
pioneer missionaries in India was extended to Ceylon. Those who
had embraced Christianity from material considerations, such as betterment in office or exemption from taxes, apostated at the first opportunity. But the dogged adherence to the faith of thousands, in
spite of two centuries of persecution under the successors of the Portuguese, shows that at least a part of the labor of the priests was not
in vain.

Many positive benefits were brought through the vehicle of the
Catholic religion. The Church paid a lot of attention to education.
The Jesuits were prominent in this respect and set up schools in the
major towns. Later there was a school attached to almost every
church. These schools taught, besides religion, which was at the center of all instruction, the Portuguese language and the child's mother
tongue. Attention was paid to the learning of Sinhalese and Tamil
because of the need to communicate with these people and to develop a Christian literature in these languages. Translations of
Christian texts in turn served to strengthen these two languages.
Tamil benefited more in this respect because of the greater volume
of work undertaken in both Ceylon and south India. The youths
who were educated in the new schools soon learned to speak Portuguese. The prevalence of this language in and around all places where
Portuguese settled made it a *lingua franca* of the Asian maritime
world. The upper classes of Ceylon were quite proficient in it, and

for a long time the Dutch communicated with the Sinhalese in this language. Portuguese also gave many new words to both Sinhalese and Tamil, especially regarding articles introduced by the Portuguese to Ceylon. These included architectural terms, furniture, articles of dress, and food. There was some miscegenation, and a new group of Eurasians came into existence with the status of a new caste. They occupied the coastal cities and continued to flourish after the Portuguese were expelled. Later colonial rulers of Ceylon depended on them, and thus Portuguese influence was perpetuated. The Catholic religion, the Portuguese language, and people of Portuguese blood outlived Portuguese power and continued as strong legacies of the half century of Portuguese occupation.

DUTCH OCCUPATION AND ITS INFLUENCES

The Kandyan kingdom under a succession of able kings not only maintained its integrity against the Portuguese but also nourished ambitions of expelling them from the island. The one great lesson of the history of the island in the sixteenth century was that only a power dominant on the seas could drive out the Portuguese. The entry of the Dutch into Indian waters in the beginning of the seventeenth century with hostile intentions against Portuguese commerce and power seemed, therefore, most timely. The two powers with a common foe lost no time in seeking each other. The first concentration of the Dutch was in the East Indian Archipelago, where they sought to monopolize the spice trade. They did not undertake any large commitment elsewhere for some time. It was only in 1638, with their power firmly entrenched at Batavia, that the long negotiations resulted in a definite alliance between the Dutch and Rajasinha II, king of Kandy. By a treaty signed in this year the Dutch promised to assist the king in his war with the Portuguese, and in return the king granted them the monopoly of the major articles of trade and a re-payment of expense incurred in the war. This treaty was similar to many others the Dutch contracted with Asian kings against the Portuguese. The kings, desperate to get rid of the Portuguese, were prepared to sign away a trade monopoly in return for necessary naval and military assistance. For the Dutch, the island's cinnamon was the great prize, for in the seventeenth century cinnamon had become a most desired spice in European trade, and its prices and sales increased immensely.

Some years of fruitful cooperation between the two allies expelled the Portuguese bit by bit from their strongholds in the island. First the east coast ports of Trincomalee and Batticaloa were taken by the Dutch and restored to the king in 1639. Then they turned their attention to the west, where the strong forts of Galle and Negombo were captured in 1640. The victorious progress of the Dutch was temporarily halted by the conclusion of a truce in Europe between the Dutch republic and the Portuguese. The truce was belatedly declared in Ceylon in 1645. In the meanwhile, serious disputes had arisen between the two allies. The king of Kandy was becoming deeply suspicious of Dutch intentions in Ceylon, as there seemed every evidence that the Dutch had decided to stay put in the places which they had captured from the Portuguese. They claimed that the king owed them large sums of money, and until this was paid they would occupy the captured towns. They set about establishing a civilian administration in the Galle area and collecting the revenues provided by these lands. When the truce ended and hostilities were resumed in 1652, the allies patched up the quarrel between themselves to get on with the immediate task of expelling the Portuguese. In the next five years, the Portuguese contested every inch of the rich cinnamon-growing lands of the southwest. Pressed by both the Dutch and the king's armies, they retreated into the heavily fortified city of Colombo. Here they desperately held out for six months, finally capitulating in May, 1656. The expedition to the north early in 1658 to annex Jaffna and Mannar was a mopping-up operation. Shortly afterward, attacks were made on the Portuguese strongholds of southern India. By the time the Dutch had finished with them, only Goa was left to the Portuguese. The superior economic resources and naval power of the Dutch enabled them to take over domination of the Indian Ocean. Particularly in the waters around southern India and Ceylon, Dutch mastery was established for a long time.

Dutch commercial policy in the East differed from that of the Portuguese. The latter had sought to control commerce by the control of strategic points through which it passed. The Dutch desired to control the areas that produced the valuable spices and thereby master their supply. Operating this policy in Ceylon, they decided very early to take over the rich cinnamon lands of the coast as well as the outlets for this spice. When the Portuguese left Colombo, the Kandyan king marched hopefully toward this place but was driven out by the Dutch. They used to advantage the debts incurred by the king and proceeded to administer and enjoy these lands until the debt should be repaid. The bill presented was so large that the king would never have been able to pay it. The king was out-maneuvered and fell a victim to his own stratagem. He had merely exchanged one foreign power for another, though he was somewhat better off now than he had been under the Portuguese. His kingdom now included the additional land he had wrested from the Portuguese in the interior while they were pressed by the Dutch on the coast. The Dutch were not interested in these lands where no cinnamon grew. He even had a few ports for his trade. Besides, the Dutch were not as quarrelsome as the Portuguese and would leave him alone as long as he left them alone. Their title was rather shaky, and, in any case, they had none of the legal claims to an all-island sovereignty by lawful succession that had been asserted by the Portuguese.

The Dutch would have been quite content to leave things in this state, but the continued hostility of the king made them take the initiative once more. Smarting under the successful Dutch maneuver, the king tried to obstruct their administration of the lowlands by inciting rebellion and systematic destruction of villages. He even toyed with the idea of getting British help against the Dutch and made certain tentative approaches to their agent in Madras. But King Rajasinha had his own troubles. There was a serious rebellion against him in 1664, which he put down with some difficulty. The Dutch took advantage of his preoccupations to carry their frontiers farther inland, acquire new districts, and form a ring around the cinnamon lands. They moved into his few remaining harbors and completely surrounded him, ensuring that no other European power would have access to him. This show of force silenced the Kandyan kings for a long time. They could not offer any noteworthy resistance, except in the internal frontier regions. But they could be a nuisance by distracting the loyalties of the Sinhalese away from the

Dutch. Thus, though there was no formal war between the Dutch and the Kandyans for a century, there was a lot of unrest in the Dutch territories. They could never achieve a real pacification of their interior dependencies because of the undercurrent of hostility of the kings of Kandy. Superficially, however, good relations existed for most of the time. The Dutch helped the kings to get their brides from southern India and their Buddhist priests from Burma. The only open war for the century and a half of Dutch occupation was in the 1760's, when, exasperated by a series of riots in the low country, the Dutch sought to put an end to this by sending an expedition to Kandy. This expedition (1762) met with the fate of similar Portuguese ventures into the hill country and was utterly routed. A succeeding one (1765) was better planned and enforced on the Kandyans a treaty conceding full Dutch sovereignty over the lowlands and making Kandy a completely landlocked kingdom.

The Dutch East India Company was a joint-stock corporation formed for the purpose of Eastern trade and now called upon to assume sovereign rights in many parts of Asia. The headquarters of their Asian administration was at Batavia, where the governor-general and his council were lodged. Under them were many subordinate administrations within and outside the Archipelago. Ceylon was the most important of their establishments outside the Archipelago, the place where they owned the most amount of territory and had the largest concentration of power. The governor was the chief executive officer and was assisted by a council of officers. His authority extended over all Dutch territories in the island and the ports along the fishery coast on the mainland across the straits. The island was subdivided into three large provinces centered around Jaffna, Colombo, and Galle. Jaffna and Galle were administered by a commander assisted by a council. In the organization of their administration, the Dutch were far superior to the Portuguese, with far greater concentration of power and responsibility and a much better machinery for consultation at every stage. The officers were paid directly from the company's treasury. The Dutch did not follow the Portuguese practice of assigning revenues from villages in payment for services. The government of Ceylon received its instructions from the Batavian government, which coordinated Dutch policy and activities in the East. But the Colombo officials had a wider measure of discretion than other subordinate governments, partly because of their distance from Batavia and partly because of their greater commitments in the island.

The framework of native administration was taken over as the Portuguese left it. As under the Portuguese, the *Dissava* of each province was the key official and was invariably a Netherlander. The other native officers—*Mudaliyars, Korles,* and *Vidanes*—were allowed to continue, with this difference: that the Dutch tried to control them more than the Portuguese did. This was motivated partly by a desire to prevent them becoming too powerful and oppressing the people. A more important reason was that the Dutch pursued clearly defined economic policies requiring a greater control over the administrative machinery. Like the Portuguese, the Dutch were faced with the problem of the doubtful loyalty of the Sinhalese nobility. They sought to get over this by enticing as many of these upper classes as possible to their Protestant faith. Those who had earlier embraced Catholicism with a view to personal betterment now found it equally easy to change to Protestantism. In this way, the Dutch were able to gather a small group of Protestant Sinhalese chiefs.

Many of the native institutions that had functioned under the Portuguese were made more efficient. The cinnamon department became even more important than before. It was headed by a Dutch officer, but the native organization was maintained. The annual demands for the European and Asian markets were calculated in advance, and the officer in charge apportioned this demand among the *chalias* (peelers) of the different villages through their headmen. The demand tended to increase every year, and it was necessary to keep the *chalia* labor force at maximum strength. Prices also tended to increase in the seventeenth century, and so the cinnamon which was collected at negligible expense from Ceylon was a great source of profit to the company. Much the same policy was adopted toward the department in charge of the capture of elephants. This was placed under a Sinhalese *Mudaliyar,* who would periodically lead parties into the woods to capture the required number of elephants. These workers traditionally held land for their maintenance. The practice of land registration was widely followed on the pattern of the Portuguese *tombo*. The native *lascarin* force was also recruited and organized in the old manner. In all these obligatory services, the demands of the state under the Dutch were found to be greater and thus a burden on the people, who were all part-time cultivators of their own land. The increase of their compulsory service to the state worked to the detriment of their fields. The Dutch met with frequent complaints, and sometimes even with riots and desertions. The *chalias* were especially discontented under the Dutch.

The Dutch encouraged the cultivation of crops that were of trade value. They made the peasants grow more pepper and cardamom. They introduced coffee into the country, but it did not catch on. Peasants had to sell these products to the state at fixed prices, and there was no incentive to greater production. The Dutch also gave attention to paddy cultivation. Swamps and marshes around Colombo were reclaimed and cultivated. A system of drainage was constructed to lead the excess water out to the sea, since flood waters were a problem in the Colombo area. The government itself undertook to plant rice and encouraged its officers to do so privately by granting them land. There was a shortage of labor, so settlement of people from south India was encouraged. In times of acute famine and distress in south India, slaves were bought and made to work on the government plantations. Toward the end of their rule, they even tried to cultivate cinnamon plantations around Colombo. All these efforts did tend to produce some progress in the agricultural economy of the coastal areas, though because of the monopolistic policies the people did not derive the fullest benefit from them.

Soon after gaining political control of the island, the Dutch sought to monopolize its trade. At first their monopoly was limited to the export of cinnamon and elephants. Later they extended it to other articles of import and export. The trade between Ceylon and south India included a number of commodities in daily use. The traders were Hindus and Muslims, living on both sides of the straits. Cloth and rice were brought to Ceylon, and areca nuts, pepper, timber, and other products were taken out. With their superior naval power and control of the seas, the Dutch had this trade at their mercy.

They took into their hands all distribution of cloth in the island and the sale of areca nuts. All who came to trade in the island had to carry Dutch passes and confine their trade to one of the larger ports—Colombo, Galle, or Jaffna. The Dutch were especially hostile to Muslim traders, who took refuge in the king's lands. After they took control of the Kandyan ports, they dominated the trade of the Kandyan kingdom as well and were then able to dictate the prices of commodities in the island. With these restrictive practices, the volume of private trade declined, and the dependence of Ceylon on south India was lessened. There was a lot of smuggling, some of it with the connivance of Dutch officers who undertook illegal private trading.

The Dutch judicial administration was a significant contribution. There were three major courts of justice—in Colombo, Jaffna, and Galle—serving the three different parts of the island. The Colombo court was also a court of appeal. The judges appointed to these courts were civil or military officials who functioned in a judicial capacity in addition to their other duties. Most of the judicial work of rural areas was carried on in the *Land Raad*, or country court, presided over by the *Dissava*. This would circulate to the various districts and was thus of easy access to the ordinary people. It invited native chiefs to sit on the court when cases involving land disputes were heard. As far as possible, the people were judged according to their own traditional laws and customs, except where these clashed violently with Dutch (Roman law) jurisprudence. As there was difficulty in ascertaining the laws of the country, the Dutch made some genuine attempts to do so. One remarkable success of these attempts was the codification of the laws and customs of the Tamils of Jaffna, the *Thesavalamai*. Dutch legal experts sat down with some *Mudaliyars* of Jaffna to codify the civil laws of that region. Thereafter, the courts administered these laws in cases involving Jaffna Tamils and have done so to the present day. For the Muslims, a code of Muslim law drafted in Batavia was applied with the approval of the Muslim headmen. No such thing was done for the Sinhalese because of the great variety of custom. Though at first they relied on the advice of the Sinhalese chiefs, the Dutch later began to apply the Roman-

Dutch law to the Sinhalese inhabitants of the cities and coastal areas, thus effecting considerable changes in property relationships among these people.

· Like the Portuguese, the Dutch tried to found a colony of their countrymen in the island. They thought they would feel safer with more of their countrymen around. So they tried to encourage people of means to come from Holland and make Ceylon their home. Men in the company's service were permitted to retire and settle down in Ceylon. This was a general policy pursued in all Dutch territories in the East. It did not succeed anywhere in the eighteenth century, for no one was prepared to emigrate from Europe to the East, certainly not men of means. The colony in Ceylon was founded by those choosing to retire from the company's service. They were granted extensive lands. Licenses for retail trading were given to them to the exclusion of others. Some were given passes to trade with the company's trading factories in India. The Burghers, as they came to be called, did not make successful farmers and very soon gravitated toward the cities, where they had more opportunities of employment. The attempt to make successful sea captains out of them was also a failure; they had not the means to set about trading in big scale, and the monopolistic policy of the Dutch debarred them from trade in the more profitable commodities. Nor was the quality of the colonists particularly good. They were generally from the lowest ranks of the military. Their general behavior in society left much to be desired. Hardly any European women settled down in Ceylon, and the colonists generally married into Portuguese families or took native wives, thus adding to the population of Eurasians in the island.

Prostestant Christianity entered the island for the first time under the Dutch. To the Dutch, religion was not as potent an influence as it was to the Portuguese. In their first zeal they took measures to root out Catholicism from the island, but the reasons were equally political as religious. Portuguese power and the Catholic religion were mutually interdependent; to be safe against one, the Dutch had to make themselves safe against the other as well. A number of laws were passed making the practice of Catholicism a serious offense and forbidding the entry of Catholic priests into the island. This was a trying time for the Catholics in Ceylon. There were no priests to minister to them. All their churches were confiscated and made into Protestant chapels. It is not surprising that all but the firm believers changed their faith and embraced Protestantism. To those who stuck doggedly to Catholicism and were prepared to run the gauntlet of Dutch persecution, the Catholic mission in India undertook a bold and clandestine ministry. They smuggled Indian priests into Dutch territories, where they were maintained underground at great risk by the parishioners. Sometimes these priests took refuge in the Kandyan lands, where the kings were far more tolerant of alien religions. In this manner, the Catholic community of coastal Ceylon succeeded in holding on until the British replaced the Dutch.

With the persecution of Catholicism came positive measures to plant Protestantism among the people. Protestant priests were recruited by the company and posted to different parts of the island. Many of the Sinhalese chiefs accepted Protestantism, at least nominally. Some Catholics were rebaptized as Protestants. But there was no effort to get to the people and preach Protestantism to them. The Dutch were not nearly as well equipped for this as the Catholics had been. Very few of their ministers knew Sinhalese or Tamil, and, in any case, there were not many of them in service in the island. No private mission could set its foot in the island; ministers were salaried servants of the company. And religion was low on the list of priorities for the company's administration of Ceylon. Some headway was made in Jaffna, where the Protestants took over the network of village churches and schools set up by the Portuguese. Tamil and Sinhalese catechists were trained to help in religious work. A certain amount of force was used to see that the baptized Christians, though not others, conformed to and practiced the faith regularly.

Education was vigorously promoted as a means to proselytization. The system initiated by the Portuguese was taken over and improved. There was a school attached to each church. The schoolmaster in charge maintained a register of attendance, and fines were imposed to ensure attendance of children. Some simple religious instruction was given, together with reading and writing in the child's vernacular and arithmetic. Regular inspection by the minister of the area and by civil officials ensured a good standard. The schoolmaster was paid by the state and also acted as registrar of births, marriages, and deaths. The introduction of a regular system of registration in the villages was a great improvement, especially the registration of marriages, which further emphasized the institution of monogamy that Christianity had sanctified. Soon the need was felt for a higher level of education. To meet this need, two seminaries were opened, in Jaffna and Colombo. Bright pupils from schools all over the country were selected and sent to one or the other of these colleges, where they were maintained and educated at state expense. Teaching was still in Sinhalese and Tamil, but some Latin and Dutch were also introduced. The purpose of this education was to equip youngsters to become teachers and catechists in the expanding school system. Toward the end of the eighteenth century, a few students were selected to receive higher education in the Netherlands. A printing press was established, and the first Sinhalese and Tamil books were printed in the island. These were translations of the Gospels and simple catechism books. The educational policy did not achieve its intended aim of spreading Christianity among the youth of the country. But it did spread literacy in the lowlands and made the people there more progressive than those in the interior.

The Dutch were more tolerant of the indigenous religions than the Portuguese had been. They prohibited Buddhist or Hindu worship in the big cities but were not concerned to root it out from the villages. There was no question, however, of returning the extensive temple property confiscated by the Portuguese. Buddhism found a comfortable home in the Kandyan kingdom, where it flourished in the seventeenth and eighteenth centuries under the watchful eyes of the Kandyan kings. Whenever the Sangha showed signs of deterioration, the ordination was revived by inviting learned priests from Burma and Siam, as happened twice in the eighteenth century. Kandy became the most important seat of Buddhism in the island, and the Temple of the Tooth erected in Kandy to house the precious tooth relic of the Buddha became the most famous Buddhist institution. Traditional learning in Pali and Sinhalese was fostered here. The eighteenth century produced some famous Sinhalese men of letters, the most outstanding of whom was Weliwita Saranankara, a name still held in reverence by the Sinhalese.

The tremendous efforts at survival of the seventeenth century and the subsequent pressure of the Dutch weakened the Kandyan kingdom, leaving it by the end of the eighteenth century an anachronistic remnant of Sinhalese power. Dutch mastery of all lucrative sources of wealth in the country left nothing with which this kingdom could rebuild itself. Its products were all channeled to Dutch ports at prices well below the market value. Land was the only source of revenue in the kingdom, and good arable land was not abundant. Communication in the mountainous terrain was very difficult, and villages and districts developed as independent economic entities, with little surplus production and no means of disposing of this surplus. Internal dynastic disputes added to its problems. In 1747 the direct Sinhalese line died out, and the throne passed to a descendant of the female line belonging to the Dravidian Nayakkar dynasty of Madura. This created tensions between a Dravidian court and a sinhalese nobility, resulting in factious disputes which later led directly to the demise of the kingdom.

Social differences which had already arisen between the Sinhalese of the low country and those of the upcountry hardened in this period. The Sinhalese of the low country, under the impact of Dutch policies, were increasingly subjected to Western influences in their social customs and laws. They enjoyed a higher standard of living and greater literacy. The Kandyans fell into an intellectual and material stagnation, knew nothing of the world around them, and were steeped in ancient tradition. Their economic organization became more feudal; chiefs, as *Dissavas* and other officers, wielded ever greater authority over the people. In spite of their declining power, the people here, especially the chiefs, kept a sense of pride, nurtured by the fact that they had retained their political independence. They naturally looked down upon the lowlanders and viewed with hostility the Christian and other Western influences to which the lowlanders had fallen prey. The Sinhalese of Ceylon had virtually divided themselves into two culturally different categories.

British Rule and Nationalist Response

By the end of the eighteenth century, the nations that had dominated the first phase of European colonization of the East had exhausted themselves. The Portuguese were restricted to a couple of trading stations, which they were permitted to keep only on account of their impotency. Their Dutch challengers had their period of commercial and naval greatness in the second half of the seventeenth century. The terrific efforts of this tiny nation to achieve such mastery seemed to have affected it considerably, and the succeeding century was one of slow but steady decline in its power. The basic cause was that the Dutch company had bitten off in the East more than it could chew. It had extended its commercial interests, naval presence, and political control far and wide, indeed, from the eastern to the western extremes of the vast Asian continent. Its officers acted more as proconsuls administering the affairs of several nationalities and conducting relations with several princes than as traders concerned with the problems of commerce. The accounting system of such a vast concern at Amsterdam was most confusing and soon lost touch with the realities of the situation. No one, not even the directors, knew the real state of the company's finances until the end of the eighteenth century, when it applied to the state for substantial loans to keep it solvent. Because of its restrictionist policies in trade, the company was making far less out of its possessions in the East than it could have, whereas the British company, with a more liberal commercial policy, was deriving utmost benefits with a much smaller outlay of capital. Corruption was rife at all levels of the Dutch administration. But the decisive considerations were the progress of the competitor nations whose trading methods were better suited to the needs of the times, and the changes in the balance of power that took place in Europe at this time.

The British East India Company, though formed at about the same time as the Dutch, had been content for a long time to concentrate solely on trade without mixing it with politics as the Dutch had done. It had centered its energies on India, where there were rich pickings if the trade was handled carefully. In the atmosphere of Indian politics in the eighteenth century, it was impossible to carry on trade unmixed with politics. The strong Moghul Empire, which had kept peace in the subcontinent for two centuries, was now in decline, and the dispersal of political power brought with it the customary lawlessness and anarchy. The immediate factor that influenced the British to take to politics in India was the bad example and threat of their rivals, the French, whose policy it was to set up puppet kings on weak thrones and exercise real power through them. The British beat the French at their own game, and the result of this Anglo-French rivalry was that the British had obtained direct control over large parts of Bengal and southern India by the end of the eighteenth century. The road to ascendancy in India was what had brought the British to Ceylon. Naval battles with the French in Indian waters again emphasized the strategic value of Ceylon, especially of Trincomalee, the natural harbor on her east coast. This provided the only safe anchorage in the Bay of Bengal when the northeastern monsoon raged in the last few months of the year, and it was an excellent base from which to control the route to eastern India and beyond. In the course of the prolonged war with France, the British occupied Trincomalee in 1782 but were forced to abandon it by the French acting in alliance with the Dutch.

The next British attempt on Ceylon was caused by the wars of the French Revolution. The revolutionary government in France overran Holland in 1794 and set up the Batavian Republic. William of Orange, the Stadholder, fled to England and refused to recognize the legality of the new government. The British feared that France, with the added strength of Holland's overseas empire, might make an attempt on their positions in India. They secured letters of authority from Prince William instructing the Dutch governor of Ceylon to admit British troops as protection against French designs. Armed with this letter, they sought admission into Trincomalee. The Dutch governor, after some hesitation, chose to resist. The British then decided to use force and expelled the Dutch from the island in 1796 with ease. At the same time, they strengthened their position by a treaty with the king of Kandy, supplanting the Dutch as protectors of the shores of Ceylon with all the privileges over trade enjoyed by the Dutch. The conquest was for the moment held to be a temporary one and solely for the protection of their Indian interests against the French. No separate administrative machinery was instituted. Ceylon was made a part of the presidency of Madras, and company officers from Madras arrived to govern the country. But as the war with France progressed, the British government was strengthened in the view that it would be foolish to give up Ceylon. Running the country from Madras was found to be unsatisfactory, and disorders had resulted from some ill-conceived changes of old customs. It was thought more advisable to bring the island directly under the Crown, both in order to give it a better government and to strengthen the chances of holding it permanently. In spite of the company's objection, Ceylon was made a crown colony in 1802. By the Peace of Amiens with France of the same year, British possession of maritime Ceylon was confirmed.

Once the British were established in maritime Ceylon, they shed completely their old reluctance to expand territorially. Quite the contrary, they were now eager to seize every opportunity to annex states and reduce kings to subjection, if these in any way threatened British interests. Under Lord Wellesley in India, they were building up a large empire by a policy of annexation and intervention. Such a policy augured ill for the continued existence of the Kandyan kingdom as an independent political entity. The British had a great deal of interest in reducing the kingdom to a subsidiary state connected to them by treaty relation, in the manner that Wellesley was subjugating many of the indigenous states of India. By following this policy in Ceylon, the expenditure of guarding all the frontier posts would be reduced. More direct access by land could be established between the western and eastern coast by building roads through the center. Trade in the produce of the highlands could be encouraged by doing away with irksome customs posts and the insecurity of conditions in Kandy. But the Kandyans would not grant any of these concessions and remained darkly suspicious of any attempt by the British to implant their influence in Kandy. The most important factor that influenced relations between these two powers was, however, the dissension within the kingdom and the intrigues that resulted. The Dravidian dynasty of Kandy was becoming increasingly unpopular, and the Sinhalese chiefs were accumulating power. The latter were jealous of the influence of the Nayakkar nobility, on whom the kings relied. Some among them even set their eyes on the throne and sought to utilize the British to achieve these objects. With this intent they started intriguing with the British, who were not averse to their overtures. The first attempt to reduce the kingdom in 1803 ended disastrously. The British had been misinformed of the extent of the king's unpopularity. Attempts by the king to tighten up his control on the kingdom, weaken the power of the chiefs, and punish those disloyal to him further increased the hostility of the chiefs. In some of these measures the king overstepped himself and aroused popular discontent as well. In 1815, the time was more opportune, the kingdom further disintegrated. A well-planned expedition, the defection of many influential nobles with their troops, and the indifference of the people to the fate of their king brought the Kandyan kingdom to its feet and ended its long independence.

All the chiefs made their formal submission to the British, and the Kandyan Convention was signed in March, 1815. It was an important document, at least from the point of view of the Kandyans, because in subsequent years they based many of their claims on its clauses. The Kandyan provinces were brought under the sovereignty of the British. The chiefs were to be maintained in the privileges accruing traditionally to their offices, and the country was to be governed according to its customary laws and institutions. An important provision guaranteed the preservation of Buddhism and its institutions within the provinces. These were guarantees thought politic for the pacification of a kingdom that hitherto no European power had reduced. The provinces were administered separately and were directly in the governor's charge. He ruled through a resident at Kandy, who virtually took the place of the monarch, and who with two others formed a board of commissioners for Kandy. Below them, the old system continued. But this situation could not last for long. There was a great incongruity between the principles on which the British administration was based and those of the Kandyan hierarchy. Reforms tending to detract from the power and influence of the chiefs were introduced with great caution. Humane reforms in judicial administration reduced the power of the chiefs, and those in the collection of revenue reduced their wealth. The *bhikkhus* also felt the effect of the disappearance of the monarch and the substitution of the patronage of an unbelieving, impartial government. They, too, were displeased with the decline in their status. This political and religious discontent came to a head, and within three years of British annexation the old order gave its last dying kick. The rebellion was popular and widespread and was put down only by great severity and repression. The proclamation of 1818, after the end of the rebellion, brought the Kandyan provinces more firmly under British control. Powers and privileges of chiefs were curtailed and British agents appointed to each province. The agent and not the chief thus became the center of provincial authority. The protection afforded to Buddhism was reduced in effect by being extended to other religions as well. By these measures, the Kandyan provinces were opened to those influences which had already been operating for a few centuries on the coast and had served to undermine the old social and economic structure. The political unification of the island was accomplished after a lapse of about six centuries.

In the first phase of British rule in Ceylon, the new masters moved cautiously, reluctant to do anything to upset the social order. The governor, who possessed all executive and legislative power, had an advisory council of the highest colonial officials. All top posts were filled by members of a civil service recruited in Britain. The governor had a lot of discretionary power, and its exercise depended on his personal ability. One of his major tasks was to see to it that the colony's budget was balanced, toward which end he was to develop all the resources of the country. But he was to do this without disrupting society and its ancient institutions. Unauthorized Europeans were not to be allowed to settle in the island. Ceylon was not to be a colony in the normally accepted sense, where a migrant population from the mother country is encouraged and given every facility. Ceylon developed as a new type of colony, whose pattern was later applied to other tropical dependencies that had a predominantly non-European population.

Yet, from the first the modernizing process was set in motion in spite of the declared intention to maintain the *status quo*. In Britain at this time a reform movement was in progress under the influence of evangelical and humanitarian ideas. This was bound to make itself felt in Ceylon. The old institution of slavery, nurtured and exploited by the Portuguese and the Dutch, was abolished by stages in the first two decades. The status and function of native officials was another matter that did not square up with the principles of British administration. They were now relieved of judicial functions to avoid the evils of concentration of power. They were paid fixed salaries in place of the assignment of revenues of villages. These reforms were extended into the Kandyan provinces after its pacification in 1818. They reduced the status of the native aristocracy and made them more dependent on the British.

One of the biggest problems of this period was the system of Rajakariya, or compulsory service, that holders of crown land owed to the state. It stood in the way of agricultural development and greater productivity, hindered the mobility of labor, and was a burden on the tenant. Its unequal incidence went against all just principles of taxation. But to recognize the malady was one thing; to remedy it was another. The system could not be scrapped forthwith, because on it depended the upkeep of some public utilities which were maintained by this labor. One important use of Rajakariya was the construction of roads and bridges. Major roads into Kandy were constructed by using compulsory labor. Various governors tried to tackle the problem piecemeal. The trend of their reforms was to substitute a grain tax for compulsory service in such a way that landlessness and impoverishment did not result. The entire system was abolished in 1832.

The British encouraged agriculture, continuing some of the experiments and methods the Dutch had inaugurated toward the end of their rule. Cinnamon and pepper plantations started by the Dutch were maintained and extended. The Dutch had experimented with coffee, without much success. With the conquest of Kandy, land more suitable for coffee was available, and in the 1820's experimental coffee plantations were opened in the hill country. The new crop promptly caught on and was extended. Sugar cane was also successfully grown in some parts. Cotton and indigo were already in existence in moderate quantities. The emphasis was thus on export crops for which there were ready markets in many parts of the world. The absence of good roads was a serious drawback to further development, and so a policy of road construction was begun. Sir Edward Barnes was the first of the great road-building governors. His road connecting Colombo with Kandy, begun in 1820, was as responsible as any other factor for the extension of plantations into the hill country. As some of these possibilities came to the fore, the early British suspicion of private European enterprise was soothed. Governors were now empowered to permit Britishers to purchase land for commercial agriculture, and these lands were readily made available. Tax exemptions and other facilities were freely granted. British officials were permitted and even encouraged to participate in this activity.

Another important influence that entered the island with British occupation was in the realm of Christian missionary education and religious activity. The liberal attitude toward private missionary activity soon attracted many missions to the island. After the London Missionary Society (1805) came in succession the Baptists (1812), the Wesleyan Methodists (1814), and the Church Mission (1818). Permission was even granted to a non-British body, the American Missionary Society, though they were not allowed to settle in Colombo but were sent to distant Jaffna (1813). All these missionary societies concentrated on education, for this was held to be the key to conversion. The government was content to leave education in the hands of the missions and to subvent them with grants. Besides being economical, it was also the way education was organized in Britain. The British government in Ceylon had no consistent policy on education, and support to the missions depended on the predilections of the governor. The missions opened and managed their own schools in various parts of the country on funds sent by home organizations. In the early years, indigenous languages were used most of the time, though some English was taught to all pupils in all the schools.

The above changes, resulting from the first phase of British rule, were haphazard and disorderly. There was no conscious colonial policy on which the British government acted. But such a policy was evolving in these very years, and the second British Empire was taking shape in the application of guiding principles of reform to the colonial sphere. In Britain, Philosophical Radicalism, as expounded by Jeremy Bentham, James Mill, and others, was a growing influence in politics. From the 1820's onward, the legal and social institutions of Britain were subjected to a thorough reform under the influence of these Utilitarian and Radical thinkers. When these philosophies were applied to the growing imperial dependencies, they gave birth to the ideal of trusteeship. These new territories were to be treated as trusts to which must be extended all that was best in the British system. A great opportunity to transform these vague ideas into concrete proposals came when a commission was appointed to look into the administrative, economic, and social conditions in the British colony of Ceylon and make recommendations. W. M. G. Colebrooke and C. H. Cameron were the members of this commission, and their report, a vital document in the history of Ceylon, is referred to as the Colebrooke Report (1831-32). It applied the principles of Benthamite Utilitarianism to every field of activity in Ceylon.

In the administrative sphere, it recommended the abolition of the existing division of the country along racial or cultural lines into low-country Sinhalese areas, Kandyan-Sinhalese areas, and Tamil areas, and the abolition of separate systems of administration to suit the needs of each area. The whole country was to be brought together under one uniform system and was to be divided on a solely territorial basis into five provinces. Colebrooke argued that catering to divisions within the country by keeping separate administrative systems only tended to perpetuate such divisions, and that the first step toward the creation of a Ceylonese nation was the administrative unification of the country. Cameron's recommendation to unify the judicial system was also to lead toward the same goal. They both recommended the gradual extension of the principles of British law to all regions and to all classes of people, so that everyone would enjoy equal rights in the eyes of the law. These measures were an exact application of the Benthamite view of legal institutions and the counterpart of the almost contemporaneous law reforms of Macaulay in India.

The commissioners were opposed to any concentration of power and viewed with alarm the autocratic powers of the governor. Many of the arbitrary judicial powers formerly held by the governor were removed. In place of the advisory council was set up an executive Council, and the government of Ceylon was henceforth to be constituted of the governor and the Executive Council. This council, enlarged by the addition of other official and unofficial nominees,

European and Ceylonese, was to form a Legislative Council to provide a forum for discussion of legislative measures. Special emphasis was placed on its Ceylonese membership as a means of informing Ceylonese public opinion, such as it was, of government policies and of ascertaining their views on contemplated legislation. This would give weight to the council's decisions and lend stability to the government. In the first Legislative Council, set up in 1833, there were nine official and six unofficial members. Three of the unofficial members were Ceylonese, nominated by the governor on a communal basis—one each to represent low-country Sinhalese, Burghers, and Tamils. To remove the exclusively British character of the administrative services, the commissioners recommended that recruitment to the civil service be open to all and that suitable Ceylonese be considered for appointment and promotion to the highest offices in the country. This provision long remained a dead letter; the executive and the civil service were the exclusive preserve of the Britisher for a good many years.

The Commissioners favored a free economy, untrammeled by state regulations and monopolies. They recommended the abolition of the monopoly of cinnamon and salt and the abandonment of state activity in other spheres of economic life. Cinnamon, coffee, and pepper plantations belonging to the state were to be sold and state export of many articles relinquished. A very important recommendation was the sale or grant of crown land in freehold to encourage development. This was to have major consequences for the future. The abolition of Rajakariya was also motived by the same basic line of thought; it would create a free labor market which the entrepreneur could use for his private ventures. Customs duties were to be reformed in a more rational manner to encourage export of the products of the country and import of articles of first necessity. The net effect of these reforms in the economic structure was to change over from the partly mercantilist concepts on which policy had so far been based to a laissez-faire concept of state. This would in turn pave the way for an increased flow of capital and increased activity by private investors who would be attracted to the island by the new policy.

The commissioners emphasized the formulation of a regular educational policy. Education must be spread to all the people if they were to comprehend new ideas and take advantage of the new facilities provided for them. The creation of a Ceylonese public opinion and its participation in the legislative process required that the people understand the new institutions and how they worked. More particularly, in order to translate into practice the accepted principle of equality of opportunity in government service at all levels, the spread and intensification of education in the English language was required. From this viewpoint, the money spent on fostering education in local languages was a waste, and the commissioners recommended the abolition of such schools run by the state. These were to be replaced by English schools all over the island. (Schools run by the missions soon fell into line with government policy and concentrated on English education.) This was another recommendation of the commission that brought some major consequences in its train. The policy was identical with reforms in India, where the famous minute of Macaulay on educational policy (1833) inaugurated a new era of British education. The management of education, as recommended by the commissioners, was left in the hands of the School Commission, consisting of Anglican clergy and government officials. This introduced missionary influence into state control of education. The system planted in Ceylon was similar to that in existence in contemporary England; the one big difference was that the majority of the people in Ceylon were non-Christians.

Basic to the above-mentioned developments were changes in the economic sphere. Due partly to independent factors and partly to the energies released by the reforms, coffee became during these years a profitable export crop. It had previously registered some limited success as a peasant crop and as a product of small plantations. But the greatest supplier to the British market was still the West Indies, and it was difficult to make a breach in their ascendancy. After the emancipation of slaves, however, the coffee estates of the West Indian colonies suffered a labor shortage, and their supplies to Britain declined. At the same time, improved methods of cultivation were brought to Ceylon from Jamaica and introduced in some of the plantations. These proved immediately successful, and large plantations were opened up by European planters. Production increased almost tenfold from 1834 to 1842. The land was crown property, sold to the planters at giveaway prices. The coffee boom continued until 1844, when it showed signs of a setback. The decline in price on the London market that began that year and continued to 1849 was related to the general economic depression that seized Britain at this time. The low prices and declining demand for Ceylon coffee was a serious blow. Many planters now found its cultivation uneconomical, and there was a possibility that many of the plantations would be closed. Thus, within a decade, coffee demonstrated the success of a boom crop and the weakness of a monocultural base to an economy.

The general economic recovery in Britain which occurred soon after had a healthy effect on the coffee culture of Ceylon. From 1849 on, prices recovered and the plantations revived. Economic management in the period of crisis had made the plantations more efficient, and the stage was set for another, more fantastic period of boom. Favored by the flourishing conditions of trade and industry in the Fifties and Sixties, the acreage under coffee increased to such proportions that it came to be know as the "coffee mania." This expansion affected not only the European planter but also the native peasant, whose holdings also were planted with coffee, especially in the neighborhood of the large plantations. The peasant crop accounted for over a quarter of the coffee exported, and thus the peasant was brought into the resultant general prosperity. But in the Seventies came the crash, a collapse as phenomenal as the rise. The cause of this crash was the spread of a disease popularly known as the coffee leaf disease. It spread rapidly from one estate to the other, drastically curtailing the annual crop. All efforts at fighting this blight were a failure. On top of this came a general fall in price in London and the growing popularity of Brazilian coffee. The evils of dependence on one crop were driven home, and the planter now started looking for means to diversify his agriculture. Cocoa, chinchona, rubber, and tea suggested themselves for experimentation. The pattern of plantation agriculture had come to stay. What were required were new and more resilient crops.

The four decades when the coffee culture was successfully carried on, imposed a certain pattern on the general economy of the country. This pattern was a lasting one and, to some extent, continues up to present times. The inflow of capital and increase of trade brought into the country the rudiments of capitalist organization. At first the majority of the planters were small capitalists who depended on loans and advances. To provide these there arose a banking system. Banks and agency houses appeared in Colombo, most of them branches of well-known foreign institutions. Business in Ceylon was drawn into the vortex of international finance. Every boom and slump in the world market was reflected in the colony, for any slight change in the price of its few export commodities vitally touched the economy. The increased sea-borne trade necessitated efficient and modern port facilities to handle large tonnage. The opening of the Suez Canal in 1869 made the harbors of Ceylon even more important, lying as they did on the highway to Australia and the Far East. In 1873, work was begun on a breakwater in Colombo to make a safe anchorage at all times of the year. After 1880, the port of Colombo entered a period of rapid expansion in traffic and trade. Within the country, the plantations were responsible for the construction of a network of roads in the plantation areas. The state now had funds, procured from the export duty on coffee, to use on this work. For the same reasons, the first railway was built in 1867, connecting Colombo and Kandy and providing cheap transport for the produce of the plantations. One by-product of faster transportation was to break down the isolation of the village and promote the unification of the country.

One of the peculiar problems created by the success of plantation agriculture was the demand and supply of labor. The freeing of the labor market by the abolition of compulsory service did not lead to the anticipated result of creating an ample labor force for economic enterprises. The fetters of the caste system and social conservatism prevented the formation of a mobile labor force. Besides, in the places where plantations tended to expand, there was no pressing economic need for the peasant to offer his labor except at rates which were unacceptable to the employers. The shortage of labor became more acute with the rapid expansion of plantations from the Thirties onward. Planting interests began to look across the straits to south India, where a steady decline in agricultural productivity in certain areas was an inducement to many Indians to migrate in search of work. At first, they were recruited seasonally, entire batches of them coming at harvest time and departing after the work was done. The conditions, both of the journey—which involved a trek on foot through jungle—and of service on the plantations, were miserable and abject, and there was a heavy death toll among the immigrants. The planters demanded that this immigration be state-sponsored. For a long time the state, maintaining its doctrinaire laissez-faire approach, was not disposed to interfere. A system was evolved by which the planters paid advances to a native agent (*Kangany*) from the Tamil areas who would contract for the supply of the required number of laborers. All expenses incurred in bringing the laborer to the plantation were treated as an advance loan to the worker, toward the clearing of which he was legally bound to work for his employer. The whole system was the grossest form of exploitation. Together with the inhuman conditions under which the laborer lived and worked, it lurked as a black background to the phenomenal growth of plantation agriculture. The labor problem, however, had been solved and a market found to provide necessary labor for all subsequent enterprises. The development of capitalism in Ceylon was spearheaded by foreign capital and foreign labor.

Out of the crops experimented with when coffee was declining, tea showed the first signs of success. It was the Indian variety, indigenous to Assam, that was introduced and did well in the hill country. The decline in the demand for China tea in Britain paved the way for greater possibilities for India tea, grown both in India and in Ceylon. Climatic conditions in the upper slopes of the hill country were found to be even more favorable to tea than in India, and in the Nineties production advanced rapidly. Unrestricted expansion could not continue into the twentieth century, because the demand for tea was an inelastic one. The British market soon became saturated, and attempts had to be made to find other markets. A drive made in the early years of the century to make Ceylon tea popular in the United States met with limited success. After the First World War, the Dutch East Indies expanded tea production, and there was a glut on the market. The marketing of tea became the monopoly of a handful of firms which resorted to blending various varieties. This hurt Ceylon and Indian tea, whose advantage was its superior quality, while the cheap Dutch East Indies variety could be used extensively in blending. All these factors led to the adoption of schemes for restricting production in Ceylon. That the Dutch East Indies refused to come into any of these schemes made the Ceylon planting interests reluctant to operate them for any length of time. The adverse effects of the Great Depression of 1929 on the world tea industry compelled the Dutch to agree to combined action. A scheme for international restriction was introduced. As the three major producers —India, Ceylon, and the Dutch East Indies—were party to it, it steadied the position of the world supply of tea.

The plantation industry was also propped up by the success of rubber in the last decades of the nineteenth century. The discovery of a species suitable to Ceylon led to its extensive cultivation from 1900 onward. An international boom in rubber in the first decade of the century favored this expansion. Most of the capital used was provided by the tea companies of the island. Ceylon did not benefit from the wide European and American investment in rubber as much as Malaya did. The priority enjoyed by tea both over capital and land curtailed the expansion of rubber planting, which was therefore slower than in Malaya. Factors similar to those that affected tea—fluctuating prices and foreign competition—affected the progress of the rubber industry as well. More of the rubber industry was in the hands of Ceylonese investors, some of it in small peasant holdings. Toward the end of British rule, Ceylonese capital in tea was only 20 per cent of the total, the rest of it being mainly European, while in rubber Ceylonese had a far greater share, their investment being 55 per cent of the total. Tea and rubber, together with coconut products, became the chief exports of the island, constituting 90 per cent of her total exports. Coconut was completely Ceylonese-owned; it was grown partly on large estates and partly on small holdings. All these products were susceptible to fluctuations caused by factors beyond the control of their producers.

In the twentieth century, immigration of labor from India was continuous and numerically greater than before. On the tea estates the nature of the demand for labor was different from that of the coffee era. There was no fixed plucking season; it was done throughout the year. The labor force had to be permanently available throughout the

year. There was thus a permanent immigrant labor population settled on the estates, though its composition changed periodically. Living quarters, of a fashion, were provided by the employers. Some of
the grosser abuses of the earlier years were remedied by legislation,
though the social welfare measures that had been adopted in Britain
were not applied to the colonies. It was more the pressure of the Indian government, in turn moved to action by public opinion in India, that moved the authorities in Ceylon to improve the system of
recruitment and conditions of service. This began a tradition of interest by the government of India in its emigrants overseas, a tradition which continued with regard to Ceylon into the period of independence. In the census of 1911, the number of Indian laborers in
Ceylon was about half a million, 12 per cent of the total population.
This ratio was maintained thereafter up to modern times. The Indian
laborers emigrated not as individuals but as entire families and even
groups of interrelated families. On the estates where they settled they
maintained this relationship and were able to reproduce in their new
environment an approximation of their native cultural pattern. They
spoke their language, worshipped their gods, and followed their customs. In their estate dwellings they had little or no contact with the
Sinhalese who lived in the villages. The separateness of their interests was recognized in the constitutional reforms of 1924, when two
members of the Indian community were nominated to the legislative
council.

The growth of the plantations did not directly affect the great mass
of the people engaged in agriculture according to the traditional
methods. Colebrooke had expected that capital would flow equally
into all forms of agriculture and lead to a general rise in the standard
of living of all sectors of the population. This did not happen, and
for a time the eyes of capitalists and officials alike were turned solely
on plantations. The rest of the country was neglected, and rice cultivation continued on the road to decline it had been taking for some
years. Nothing was done to improve irrigation; the traditional means
of maintaining the works were upset by the reforms of Colebrooke.
The opening of plantations had adverse consequences on the peasants of the highlands. The indiscriminate sale of what was held to be
crown land took no account of the customary law of the land or of

needs of the people. Much of the hilly jungle land claimed as crown land and sold to the planters had been used by the peasants to graze their cattle and to grow highland crops for their sustenance. Peasant discontent, over these things and over some new taxes introduced by the government, caused the civil riots of 1848. These riots drew the attention of the government to the peasant problem. From the sixties the state started to spend money on the repair of some ancient major irrigation works and many smaller ones. Neglected centers of early civilization in the north-central and eastern provinces again became the scenes of government activity. While earlier these areas had been left behind in the road construction program, they were now made more accessible by trunk roads. The railway to the north opened up many of these parts. The extension of medical facilities to these areas improved the general health of the people. In spite of these activities, however, there was a big difference between the standards of living, ways of life, and attitudes of the peasantry in these areas and those of the peasants in the coastal lands, who had been more closely subjected to the influences of capitalism and Western rule.

Next to economic factors, education was a great source of influence and change in society. English education caught on among the upper classes, and missionary educational enterprise was widened. It was soon found impractical to neglect Sinhalese and Tamil altogether. So education became bilingual, more of the pupil's mother tongue being used at the primary level and more of English at the later stages. A system of grants-in-aid started in 1870 had increased the number of missionary schools, which were now open in every sizable town of the island. The government confined itself to opening vernacular schools in places not served by the missionaries. The products of the English schools were absorbed in clerical employment either in government or in large private companies. In the twentieth century, when some of the earlier assumptions of liberalism were being questioned, a greater emphasis was placed by the government on vernacular education. But the English schools were far better equipped and gave better education; vernacular education was confined to remote rural areas or to the children of the lowest classes in society. In the sphere of higher education, connections were at first maintained with Indian universities. A college was established in 1921 to prepare for examinations of the University of London. The curriculum of schools was consequently oriented toward Western culture. Western classics, English literature, and Western history were emphasized. The students knew little or nothing of their own literature, history, or institutions. Education was not just in the medium of English; its subject matter was also westernized.

One of the most significant social consequences of the educational system was the emergence of a new class which cut across the traditional division of society into caste groups on a functional basis. At the topmost level of this new class was the Ceylonese entrepreneur who had taken advantage of the recent economic innovations. He had invested in rubber or coconut, set up as contractor for the numerous constructions, made his money in road haulage, or set up import-export agencies. Next came the professional men, who, having undergone training either in Ceylon or in Britain, were successful practitioners in Colombo and other major towns. Then there were the Ceylonese members of the administrative services, divided into the executive and clerical grades. The executive grades of the administration had been barred to Ceylonese for a long time, but in the twentieth century, with the rapid expansion of education at higher levels, these also were thrown open, and the Ceylonese entered the sanctified ranks of the civil service. The clerical grades were far more numerous. With the increase in the number of government departments came an increase in the demand for men to fill clerical posts; such clerical hands were required in the private sector as well. Recruits came directly from secondary school. Another substantial group included in the new class were the schoolmasters. Though drawn from different economic strata, all these groups are referred to as a middle class because they bore certain common characteristics. Almost all of them had enjoyed an English education, though at different levels. They were proficient in the use of the English language, which had opened to them the new world of Western learning and ideas. Both consciously and unconsciously, they had adopted the scientific, rational outlook on life which now influenced their attitude to the society in which they moved. More concretely, they had adopted European dress and modes of living. This progressive and forward-looking class became the focus of developments in twentieth-century Ceylon.

The public opinion and political life that Colebrooke envisaged had to await the growth of the Ceylonese middle class. For a greater part of the nineteenth century, political controversy in Ceylon, within and without the Legislative Council, was waged on how far the state should fall in with the demands of the European planting interests. The unofficial European members constituted the opposition and put forward a demand to have a majority of unofficial members in the council that was rejected by the colonial government. When Ceylonese opinion did show signs of emerging, it was, as in India, on the social, religious, and educational fronts. The first energies of nationalist consciousness were directed toward reforming the old religions and society. Revivalist movements in Buddhism and Hinduism undertook a more scientific study and presentation of the tenets of their faith. They realized the urgency of modernizing their institutions so that they could be in a position to resist the inroads of Christianity. Buddhist and Hindu schools were established to impart English education of a high standard unmixed with the Christian religion. The rediscovery and publication of old texts and an emphasis on their Eastern heritage was an important aspect of the new education. This movement was greatly helped by European philologists and historians, who took an interest in Ceylon's past and unearthed, by their new tools of research, many aspects of its civilization which had been hidden for centuries. The archeological work at Anuradhapura and Polonnaruwa and the exposure of an indisputedly great civilization fed the national consciousness. Sporadic attempts were initiated to reform some of the evils in society. Temperance movements of the Eighties sought to eradicate drunkenness. The Ceylon Social Reform Society was founded in 1905, partly to reform the old abuses and partly to resist further westernization of middle class society.

This national consciousness very soon made itself felt in the political plane. Already by the end of the nineteenth century, individual middle class Ceylonese, as nominated members of the Legislative Council, were making their voice felt in political questions. Associations of a regional or communal character soon grew up in the educationally more advanced parts of the country. The unanimity of the demands put forward by these individual groups reflects the common ideologies which influenced their thinking. All of them petitioned the colonial government for constitutional reform embodying a measure of power for the Ceylonese people in the executive, a wider representation on a territorial basis in the legislative, and application of the elective principle to replace the practice of nomination by the governor. In contrast with the demands and methods of agitation of the Indian nationalist movement of this time, these demands were exceedingly moderate. But the Indians had succeeded in unifying their nationalist agitation under the Congress as early as 1882; the Ceylonese had not yet done so. The British government did not, therefore, feel pressed to give concessions to the nationalist movement. The governor rejected the claims of the nationalists to speak for the mass of the Ceylonese population. He declared that the nationalists were a tiny group of middle class malcontents, totally unrepresentative of rural Ceylon. This was to be the imperial line of approach in both India and Ceylon for some years. The constitutional reforms of 1910 thus retained the old structure, with an executive controlled by the governor and an official majority in the legislature. The only change was a limited recognition of the elective principle when an electorate of "educated Ceylonese," drawn on a high educational qualification from all over the island, was set up. This electorate could send one member to the Legislative Council. As for the rest, the old principle of nomination by communities was retained.

The war of 1914-18 was an important influence on the growth of nationalism in Ceylon. The statement of aims by the Allies, propagated all over the world, concerning the right of small nations to freedom had its effect on the nationalists of Ceylon. The principle of self-determination on which the subsequent peace was held to be based was taken by the nationalists to apply to Ceylon as well. Civil riots that took place in 1915, unconnected with any political problem, served to bring to the fore the need for political organization by the nationalists. These were communal riots between Sinhalese and Muslims in the western province, and they caused the government to panic and take stern measures against the leaders of the majority community. Indiscriminate arrests and detentions brought in some respected Sinhalese citizens, including Mr. D. S. Senanayake, a mild, respectable, and very loyal country gentleman who had actually used his influence to stop the rioting. The agitation for their release, led by Mr. (later Sir) P. Ramanathan, a Tamil political leader and elected member of the Legislative Council, was one of the earliest attempts at political activity against the actions of the government. It provoked people like Mr. Senanayake, who had so far not taken an interest in politics, to enter the arena of nationalist politics. It convinced nationalist elements of the need for coordinated agitation if they were to make a mark on the colonial government.

This was the background to the formation of the Ceylon National Congress in 1919, uniting the major Sinhalese and Tamil organizations. The influence and example of the Indian nationalist movement was clear. It was only in 1916 that the Congress and Muslim League had come together at Lucknow to present a unified demand for reform. The result had been the declaration of 1917 and the subsequent steps taken to give effect to its aim of the "progressive realization of responsible government in India." The obvious lesson in Ceylon was this: unless Ceylonese nationalism became more national and less partisan, no major constitutional advance could be expected. The Congress quickly drafted a proposal for a new constitution and submitted it to the imperial government. Their constitution provided for a legislature (with a territorially elected majority) with control over the budget and an executive partially constituted of members drawn from the legislature. It represented a major advance from the existing constitution of 1910, yet it would have been a most cumbersome one to operate. The colonial government, while retaining responsibility for ruling the island, would have abdicated power to a legislature which had only a partial control over the executive.

The constitution granted in 1920 and modified slightly in 1924 went some way toward meeting nationalist demands. It granted an outright unofficial majority. The number of territorially elected members was increased to 23, and those who had hitherto been nominated to represent communities were to be elected by communal electorates. This greatly increased the representative element in the legislature and brought the colony to the stage of representative government. The nationalist demand for representation in the executive was rejected; the executive remained in the control of the governor and executive Council of top officials and others not connected with the legislature. The unofficial members of the Legislative Council together with three officials formed a finance committee which could examine the budget. This was as near as the elected representatives got to the control of power. In the absence of actual exercise of executive power, they made use of this committee to delve into administrative problems. They had the right to call for the appearance of heads of departments, a right which they used freely. As they had no responsibility for the exercise of executive power, their activities were looked upon by the officials as irresponsible and sometimes ill-advised. The basic defect of this constitution was the divorce of power from responsibility; an elected legislature had the power to interfere with the execution of policies for which it had no responsibility. This defect was inherent in the stage of constitutional evolution in which the colony found itself. The crown colony system—with an executive responsible to London and run by British officials who used the legislature as a sounding board of public opinion, a mere arm of the executive—had ceased to exist in Ceylon. The legislature had been vested with substantial power and had come under the control of nationalist politicians. The next stage was obviously one in which the leaders of the legislature must be given representation in the executive. How was this to be done without impairing imperial control and imperial interests? This was the problem the Donoughmore commissioners were sent to tackle.

The Ceylonese nationalists were dissatisfied with the constitution offered by Governor Manning in 1920. The National Congress agreed to cooperate in its working only with the greatest reluctance. Besides the denial of a share of responsibility in the executive, the retention of communal electorates also incensed them. They saw in this an insidious attempt to divide the people and used against it the same arguments that were used by their counterparts in India. The full recognition of territorial representation and abolition of communal electorates would have benefited the majority community and increased their representation in the legislature. As the minorities realized this, their leaders who had joined the Congress to present a united front now broke away. The most influential minority community, the Tamils, formed their own organization to agitate for the interests of their community. The Congress became an organization of the Sinhalese of the low country. None of the nationalist groups ever engaged in mass political activity. The National Congress was dominated by men of property and the Tamil organizations by professional men. Their attention was absorbed in disputes over representation in the legislature and in the work of its various committees.

The commission, with Lord Donoughmore as chairman, to examine the constitution of Ceylon and make recommendations for its revision visited Ceylon at the end of 1927 and reported to the colonial secretary in the middle of 1928. Most of these recommendations were embodied in a new constitution that was inaugurated in 1931. The commission criticized the 1924 constitution on the ground that it neither provided the island with a strong executive nor furnished the elected representatives with an opportunity to grapple with the problems of government. They noted that in many subcommittees irresponsible criticism and preoccupation with trivial details of administration resulted from this rigid separation of the executive from the legislature. They recognized that the time had come when the Ceylonese leaders ought to be given a share of real power so that they might benefit from the hard school of experience and learn the workings of a parliamentary system. They were convinced from their contacts with these leaders that there was ample material from which the country's political progress could be realized. What was required was a constitution that would channel their energies along constructive and fruitful lines. This would prepare them for the assumption of full responsibility for their own affairs that they were, no doubt, envisaging.

As the next constitutional commission testified 14 years later, the Donoughmore Constitution was most successful in its declared aims of providing training for self-government. This it did by introducing some bold and radical changes. The first and most important problem was to devise a constitution giving real power to the Ceylonese people and at the same time providing for the exercise of ultimate responsibility by the Imperial Government. The constitution adopted was ingeniously designed to achieve some of these aims. The division between executive and legislature was dispensed with, and the State Council, a body with an overwhelming majority of territorially elected members, functioned both in executive and legislative capacities. For executive work it was divided into seven committees, each electing its own chairman. These chairmen would be called ministers. All ministers came together in a board for coordinating their activities and presenting the annual budget. Three officials were members of this board and managed those affairs that were reserved for the governor's control. The subjects that came under the jurisdiction of the seven elected ministers and their committees covered the whole ground of internal administration. This executive committee system was a break away from the cabinet system that had evolved in Britain and which the British had so far been introducing in their self-governing dominions. In the absence of a developed party system, an executive collectively responsible to a legislature and commanding a permanent majority in it was impossible. Besides, the executive committee system had the advantage of associating as many of the elected members as was possible in the administration of the country. Members of a committee, together with the chairman, specialized in the administration of departments that came within their province.

With regard to representation, the constitution abolished communal electorates and substituted a wholly territorial system in which the country was divided into electorates with consideration to population and area. All minority communities opposed this, because the weight they had possessed under the former system would now disappear. The Donoughmore commissioners argued that representation on communal lines would perpetuate communalism and obstruct the formation of political groupings or the consideration of political issues on noncommunal lines. The minorities, especially the Tamils, were alarmed at the prospect of the British handing more power to the people of Ceylon without safeguards for the communal minority groups against a permanent Sinhalese majority. Their fears were discounted by the Donoughmore commissioners and later by the Soulbury commissioners. Both commissions favored a territorial system of representation that resulted in a substantial Sinhalese majority in the legislature. The Tamils, after an initial period of futile boycott of the 1931 constitution, entered the State Council and co-operated with Sinhalese leaders.

Another bold step forward in the matter of representation was the introduction of universal suffrage in 1931. The previously existing franchise, by imposing a high property and educational qualification, gave the vote to about four per cent of the population. The decision to enfranchise the entire adult population was again influenced by the desire to provide the maximum opportunities for political education and broaden the basis of political power. Since it had been decided to transfer power to the Ceylonese by stages, it was important to ensure that power was not seized and retained by an oligarchy.

The constitution of 1931 served Ceylon for over 15 years, through the difficult period of the Second World War. Ceylonese politicians took full advantage of the Executive Committee system. Able men were thrown into ministerial positions, gaining valuable experience in the process. Even back-benchers were able to participate in government and influence policy to a degree they could not have done in a cabinet system. No doubt, the absence of coordination was an inherent defect of the system, as each committee worked independently and the board of ministers was collectively responsible only for the budget. After a few years, the board overcame this defect by increasingly taking on the aspect of a Cabinet. One of the most fruitful innovations was the adult franchise. Its immediate result was shown in a far greater concern for social welfare than hitherto among nationalist leaders. This concern was reflected in an extensive welfare legislative program in the State Council. Health services, the educational system, and labor relations were revolutionized. It also led to the growth of a radical and socialist group of nationalist politicians who, though a minority, played an important role in provoking government concern for the common man. It is also true that communalism in politics received a setback with the emergence of economic and social issues. From the British point of view, the chief merit of the constitution was that it worked without mishap during the war.

Unlike the Indian nationalists, who demanded a guarantee of independence before they would cooperate in the war effort (and therefore spent the war years in jail), the Ceylonese leaders threw themselves wholeheartedly behind the British. The loss of Singapore to the Japanese in February, 1942, made Ceylon the nearest base for operations in Southeast Asia. Colombo and Trincomalee were again invested with strategic importance, as they had been so often in past colonial history. A commander-in-chief was appointed to take over responsibility for the island's defense, with complete power over civil administration. He did not find it necessary to use his dictatorial powers. The board of ministers was most cooperative, and civil administration was carried out through existing channels. But the leaders were not politically idle during this period. Though there was no question of agitation, they privately pressed the British for a reform of the constitution. By the middle of 1943, the worst period of the war was over, and the British were taking the offensive. A declaration issued by the secretary of state for colonies in 1943 promised full responsible government, subject to certain conditions relating to defense and external affairs. When the war was won, a commission would be appointed to examine the proposals of the Ceylonese ministers and recommend a new constitution. Though this offer fell short of dominion status, Mr. D. S. Senanayake, the leader of the State Council, was prepared to take it up. From this decision followed a trail of negotiations and discussions that set in motion the progress toward the final stage of constitutional development.

There are few general works of any quality on Ceylon. Historians have concentrated on particular periods or particular aspects, of which there is still much pioneering effort to be done. The few attempts at a comprehensive general history have revealed many gaps in our knowledge of Ceylon's past. H. W. Codrington's *A Short History of Ceylon* (rev. ed., London: 1947) relates a continuous story from the early beginnings to 1833. It is valuable for the amount of factual information it brings together, though some of it has been rendered obsolete by later research. Sydney D. Bailey's *Ceylon* was written for the Hutchinson's "University Library Series" (London: 1952). It emphasizes the period of Western impact to the neglect of the earlier periods in the history of Ceylon. The most successful attempt at a general history is E. F. C. Ludowyk, *The Story of Ceylon,* in the "Story" series of Faber and Faber (London: 1962). It takes full advantage of the great advances in historical research in the preceding decade and is presented in a form that will interest both the general reader and the student of history. B. H. Farmer's monograph, *Ceylon: A Divided Nation* (London: 1963) ranges over Ceylon's past, picking out those aspects he holds responsible for the contemporary situation.

Works dealing with large periods in outline are more common. They have generally followed the obvious lines of division: ancient and medieval to the sixteenth century, Portuguese, Dutch, and British periods. G. C. Mendis, *Early History of Ceylon* (Calcutta: 1932), was among the first works to treat the pre-European period in a critical way. It held the field for a long time as the only work of its kind, until the appearance of *A Concise History of Ceylon* by C. W. Nicholas and S. Paranavitana

(Colombo: 1961). This is an authoritative work on the centuries before the arrival of the Portuguese and embodies much original research. It is strongest on cultural history. The European periods are better provided with textbooks and outline histories. Fr. S. G. Perera's *History of Ceylon for Schools* (Colombo: n.d.), divided into three parts (Portuguese, Dutch and British), is a continuous narrative of main events. P. E. Pieris, *Ceylon: The Portuguese Era* (2 vols., Colombo: 1913-14), is a detailed survey of Portuguese activities on the island with rather more emphasis on military and diplomatic history than on economic and social aspects. The same author's *Ceylon and the Hollanders 1658-1798* (Colombo: n.d.) is not as good. The best general work on the British period is still G. C. Mendis, *Ceylon Under the British* (3rd ed., Colombo: 1952). It brings out British influences with clarity and reviews the constitutional progress of the island to 1943.

The serious student of Ceylon's history must look at the sources on which most of the histories are based. The earliest of these are the Pali chronicles of the Sinhalese. The *Mahavamsa* (Colombo: 1912) and the *Chulavamsa*, in two parts (1929-30), have been translated and edited by Wilhelm Geiger. These three volumes, written by three Buddhist monks, relate the story of the Sinhalese line of kings. They take us into the world of the ideas, beliefs, and assumptions of ancient and medieval Buddhism. The 1950 reprint of the *Mahavamsa* has an addendum by G. C. Mendis incorporating later research. In the same category of historical writing is Father Fernao de Queyroz's Portuguese account, *The Temporal and Spiritual Conquest of Ceylon*, written in 1687. It is a monumental work in six books, translated and edited by Fr. S. G. Perera in three volumes (Colombo: 1930). It covers the history of Portuguese conquest, administration, and loss of Ceylon in great detail and with refreshing candor, though from the point of view of a Jesuit missionary. All modern histories of the Portuguese are based on Queyroz. In the category of descriptive works, the most valuable as a source is Robert Knox's *An Historical Relation of the Island Ceylon* (London: 1681). An English merchant engaged in Asian trade, he was stranded off the east coast of Ceylon, where he was taken captive by the king of Kandy, and he remained there for 18 years (1660-79). His account of the Kandyan provinces is our only source of information for the economic organization and social conditions of this region. For the rest of the island in the seventeenth and eighteenth centuries, there are a number of memoirs of Dutch governors, each one a general statement of the position in Ceylon prepared for the guidance of his successor. Some of these have been translated from the Dutch and published. To get an idea of the problems that were uppermost in the minds of the administrators of that time, the student may look at two of the most instructive of these: *Memoirs of Ryckloff van Goens, 1663-1675*, translated by E. Reimers (Colombo: 1932), and *Memoir of Jan Schreuder 1757-1762*, also translated by Reimers (Colombo: 1946). They are both in the series known as "Selections From the Dutch Records of the Ceylon Government," in which other memoirs and records of interest have been published. In the British period the *Colebrooke-Cameron Report* has published in two volumes, together with other relevant despatches and an introduction by G. C. Mendis (London: 1956). The introduction relates the proposed reforms to the broader setting of British colonial policy and discusses their importance to future development. In the sphere of constitutional development, there are the Donoughmore Report (London: 1928) and the Soulbury Report (London: 1945), each with the title *Ceylon: Report of the Special Commission on the Constitution*. They are both tersely written documents analyzing critically the problems faced by the island in its constitutional progress.

There is a growing body of specialist literature on Ceylon. For a long time, research into Ceylon's history was weighted on the side of the European periods, as sources were more abundant and more readily available. In recent years, however, the ancient heritage has been looked into more and more. Much of the work has taken the form of theses for higher degrees, many of which are as yet unpublished. A great deal is being published that is of value and that adds significantly to our understanding of the past.

One of the best accounts of medieval Sinhalese civilization is Wilhelm Geiger's *Culture of Ceylon in Medieval Times* (Wiesbaden: 1960). It was written in 1940 by a famous German Indologist as one of his final works, but it was not published for twenty years. It is a remarkable study of the social history of the Sinhalese from the fourth to the fifteenth centuries A.D. The work has been edited by Heinz Bechert, who adds footnote references to later research on subjects dealt with in the book. In the field of social history there is also M. B. Aryapala, *Society in Medieval Ceylon* (Colombo: 1956), based mainly on medieval Sinhalese literature. Walpola Rahula's *History of Buddhism in Ceylon* (Colombo: 1956) provides a critical history of the establishment and progress of Buddhism in Ceylon up to the tenth century A.D. The history of Sinhalese art is well covered. S. Paranavitana, a well-known archaeologist and historian of Ceylon, has been responsible for much work in this field. His

The Stupa in Ceylon (Colombo: 1946) and *Art and Architecture of Ceylon, Polonnaruwa Period* (Colombo: 1954) cover Sinhalese art quite comprehensively. Ananda K. Coomaraswamy, *Medieval Sinhalese Art* (2nd ed., New York: 1956) is another classic on the subject. Specifically on Sinhalese sculpture, there is D. T. Devendra, *Classical Sinhalese Sculpture c.300 B.C. to A.D. 1000* (London: 1958), giving a controversial view of the origin of the Buddha image. For the history of literature, G. P. Malalasekera, *The Pali Literature of Ceylon* (London: 1928), and C. E. Godakumbure, *Sinhalese Literature* (Colombo: 1955), are standard works in their respective fields. A noted contribution in gathering the most recent researches into ancient and medieval Ceylon was made with the publication of *History of Ceylon* Vol. I, Part 1 (Colombo: 1959) and Part 2 (1960), a cooperative work to which many scholars have contributed on their special fields.

The comparative inaccessibility of the Lisbon archives has led to the almost total absence of any specialist studies on specific problems in the Portuguese period. For the period of Dutch occupation a beginning has been made with K. W. Goonewardena, *The Foundation of Dutch Power in Ceylon, 1638-1658* (Amsterdam: 1958), and S. Arasaratnam, *Dutch Power in Ceylon, 1658-1687* (Amsterdam: 1958), both using Dutch records from the archives of The Hague. There is no such study for the eighteenth century. There is, however, a penetrating examination of Kandyan society from the sixteenth to the eighteenth centuries by a sociologist, Ralph Pieris, in *Sinhalese Social Organisation* (Colombo: 1956). The first phase of British rule in Ceylon has been brilliantly reviewed in Colvin R. de Silva, *Ceylon Under the British Occupation, 1795-1832* (2 vols., Colombo: 1942). It is a study of British policy and its impact in the political, administrative, economic, and social spheres. For administrative history, there is Lennox Mills, *Ceylon Under British Rule, 1795-1832* (London: 1933). From this point to the end of the century there is a gap. It is only when we come to the twentieth century that major writings treat the subject. S. Namasivayam, *The Legislatures of Ceylon* (London: 1951), traces the evolution of the legislative councils of Ceylon through their various stages until independence. I. D. S. Weerawardana, *Government and Politics in Ceylon (1935-1946)*, (Colombo: 1951) is a study of the Donoughmore Constitution. Sir Ivor Jennings, *The Constitution of Ceylon* (3rd ed., London: 1953), analyzes the constitution of independent Ceylon, giving the "inside" story of how it came into being. The same author's *The Economy of Ceylon* (2nd ed., London: 1951) is a well-written survey of the island's economy at about the time of independence. Among works on independent Ceylon, W. Howard Wriggins, *Ceylon: Dilemmas of a New Nation* (Princeton: 1960) is the most outstanding. It is a classic analysis of trends in Ceylon since independence, their causes, their interrelation, and their consequences. It shows a rare mastery of the essentials of Ceylonese politics in contemporary times.

Of current journals there are two which contain articles of interest to the student of history and the social sciences: *The Journal of the Ceylon Branch of the Royal Asiatic Society*, and *The Ceylon Journal of Historical and Social Studies*.

INDEX